Workshop on Semantic Parsing 2014

(SP14)

Held at ACL 2014

Baltimore, Maryland, USA
26 June 2014

ISBN: 978-1-63439-204-4

Printed from e-media with permission by:

Curran Associates, Inc.
57 Morehouse Lane
Red Hook, NY 12571

Some format issues inherent in the e-media version may also appear in this print version.

Printed by Curran Associates, Inc. (2014)

For permission requests, please contact the Association for Computational Linguistics
at the address below.

Association for Computational Linguistics
209 N. Eighth Street
Stroudsburg, Pennsylvania 18360

Phone: 1-570-476-8006
Fax: 1-570-476-0860

acl@aclweb.org

Additional copies of this publication are available from:

Curran Associates, Inc.
57 Morehouse Lane
Red Hook, NY 12571 USA
Phone: 845-758-0400
Fax: 845-758-2634
Email: curran@proceedings.com
Web: www.proceedings.com

Introduction

Semantic parsers map sentences to formal representations of their underlying meaning. Recently, algorithms have been developed to learn to recover increasingly expressive representations with ever weaker forms of supervision. These advances have enabled many applications, including question answering, relation extraction, robot control, interpreting instructions, and generating programs.

This workshop, collocated with ACL 2014, aims to achieve two goals. First, to bring together researchers in the field to discuss the state of the art and opportunities for future research. Second, to create a stage for presenting the variety of current approaches, thereby providing a unique opportunity for new entrants to the field.

Organizers:

Yoav Artzi, University of Washington
Tom Kwiatkowski, Allen Institute for AI
Jonathan Berant, Stanford University

Steering Committee:

Percy Liang, Stanford University
Jakob Uszkoreit, Google
Luke Zettlemoyer, University of Washington

Program Committee:

Gabor Angeli, Stanford University
John Blitzer, Google
Johan Bos, University of Groningen
Qingqing Cai, Temple University
Stephen Clark, Cambridge University
Dipanjan Das, Google
Anthony Fader, University of Washington
Nicholas FitzGerald, University of Washington
Dan Goldwasser, The University of Maryland
Karl Moritz Hermann, University of Oxford
Chloe Kiddon, University of Washington
Jayant Krishnamurthy, Carnegie Mellon University
Nate Kushman, Massachusetts Institute of Technology
Mike Lewis, The University of Edinburgh
Smaranda Muresan, Columbia University
Hoifung Poon, Microsoft Research
Siva Reddy, The University of Edinburgh
Matthew Richardson, Microsoft Research
Dan Roth, University of Illinois at Urbana-Champaign
Andreas Vlachos, University of Cambridge
Alexander Yates, Temple University
Mark Yatskar, University of Washington

Invited Speakers:

Kevin Knight, University of Southern California / Information Sciences Institute
Percy Liang, Stanford University
Raymond Mooney, The University of Texas at Austin
Hoifung Poon, Microsoft Research
Mark Steedman, The University of Edinburgh
Stefanie Tellex, Brown University
Luke Zettlemoyer, University of Washington

Sponsored by Google

Table of Contents

Learning a Lexicon for Broad-coverage Semantic Parsing
James Allen 1

Semantic Parsing using Distributional Semantics and Probabilistic Logic
Islam Beltagy, Katrin Erk and Raymond Mooney 7

Large-scale CCG Induction from the Groningen Meaning Bank
Sebastian Beschke, Yang Liu and Wolfgang Menzel 12

Semantic Parsing for Text to 3D Scene Generation
Angel Chang, Manolis Savva and Christopher Manning 17

A Deep Architecture for Semantic Parsing
Edward Grefenstette, Phil Blunsom, Nando de Freitas and Karl Moritz Hermann 22

Combining Formal and Distributional Models of Temporal and Intensional Semantics
Mike Lewis and Mark Steedman 28

Cooking with Semantics
Jonathan Malmaud, Earl Wagner, Nancy Chang and Kevin Murphy 33

Representing Caused Motion in Embodied Construction Grammar
Ellen K Dodge and Miriam R L Petruck 39

Low-Dimensional Embeddings of Logic
Tim Rocktäschel, Matko Bošnjak, Sameer Singh and Sebastian Riedel 45

Software Requirements: A new Domain for Semantic Parsers
Michael Roth, Themistoklis Diamantopoulos, Ewan Klein and Andreas Symeonidis 50

From Treebank Parses to Episodic Logic and Commonsense Inference
Lenhart Schubert 55

On maximum spanning DAG algorithms for semantic DAG parsing
Natalie Schluter 61

Intermediary Semantic Representation through Proposition Structures
Gabriel Stanovsky, Jessica Ficler, Ido Dagan and Yoav Goldberg 66

Efficient Logical Inference for Semantic Processing
Ran Tian, Yusuke Miyao and Takuya Matsuzaki 71

Towards README-EVAL : Interpreting README File Instructions
James White 76

Freebase QA: Information Extraction or Semantic Parsing?
Xuchen Yao, Jonathan Berant and Benjamin Van Durme 82

Workshop Program

Thursday, June 26, 2014

9:00–9:05 Opening Remarks

Invited Talks

9:05–9:50 *Semantic Parsing: Past, Present, and Future*
Raymond Mooney

9:50–10:20 *Can a Machine Translate Without Knowing What Translation Is?*
Kevin Knight

Exceptional Submission Talks

10:20–10:30 *Low-Dimensional Embeddings of Logic*
Tim Rocktäschel, Matko Bošnjak, Sameer Singh and Sebastian Riedel

10:30–11:00 Coffee Break

11:00–11:10 *Combining Formal and Distributional Models of Temporal and Intensional Semantics*
Mike Lewis and Mark Steedman

11:10–11:20 *Cooking with Semantics*
Jonathan Malmaud, Earl Wagner, Nancy Chang and Kevin Murphy

11:20–12:30 **Poster Session**

Learning a Lexicon for Broad-coverage Semantic Parsing
James Allen

Semantic Parsing using Distributional Semantics and Probabilistic Logic
Islam Beltagy, Katrin Erk and Raymond Mooney

Large-scale CCG Induction from the Groningen Meaning Bank
Sebastian Beschke, Yang Liu and Wolfgang Menzel

Semantic Parsing for Text to 3D Scene Generation
Angel Chang, Manolis Savva and Christopher Manning

Thursday, June 26, 2014 (continued)

Leveraging Frame Semantics and Distributional Semantics for Unsupervised Semantic Slot Induction in Spoken Dialogue Systems
Yun-nung Chen, William Yang Wang and Alexander Rudnicky

Semantic Parsing for Information Extraction
Eunsol Choi, Tom Kwiatkowski and Luke Zettlemoyer

Parsing and Grounding Referring Expressions in Automatically Constructed 3D Models
Nicholas Fitzgerald and Luke Zettlemoyer

Graph-Based Algorithms for Semantic Parsing
Jeffrey Flanigan, Samuel Thomson, David Bamman, Jesse Dodge, Manaal Faruqui, Brendan O'Connor, Nathan Schneider, Swabha Swayamdipta, Chris Dyer and Noah A. Smith

A Deep Architecture for Semantic Parsing
Edward Grefenstette, Phil Blunsom, Nando de Freitas and Karl Moritz Hermann

Symmetry-Based Semantic Parsing
Chloé Kiddon and Pedro Domingos

Leveraging Heterogeneous Data Sources for Relational Semantic Parsing
Meghana Kshirsagar, Nathan Schneider and Chris Dyer

Context-dependent Semantic Parsing for Time Expressions
Kenton Lee, Yoav Artzi, Jesse Dodge and Luke Zettlemoyer

Combining Formal and Distributional Models of Temporal and Intensional Semantics
Mike Lewis and Mark Steedman

Cooking with Semantics
Jonathan Malmaud, Earl Wagner, Nancy Chang and Kevin Murphy

Representing Caused Motion in Embodied Construction Grammar
Ellen K Dodge and Miriam R L Petruck

Constructing Semantic Parsing Datasets from Technical Documentation
Kyle Richardson and Jonas Kuhn

Notes on the MCTest Dataset for the Open-Domain Machine Comprehension of Text
Matthew Richardson, Christopher J.C. Burges and Erin Renshaw

Thursday, June 26, 2014 (continued)

Low-Dimensional Embeddings of Logic
Tim Rocktäschel, Matko Bošnjak, Sameer Singh and Sebastian Riedel

Software Requirements: A new Domain for Semantic Parsers
Michael Roth, Themistoklis Diamantopoulos, Ewan Klein and Andreas Symeonidis

From Treebank Parses to Episodic Logic and Commonsense Inference
Lenhart Schubert

On maximum spanning DAG algorithms for semantic DAG parsing
Natalie Schluter

Intermediary Semantic Representation through Proposition Structures
Gabriel Stanovsky, Jessica Ficler, Ido Dagan and Yoav Goldberg

Efficient Logical Inference for Semantic Processing
Ran Tian, Yusuke Miyao and Takuya Matsuzaki

A New Corpus for Context-Dependent Semantic Parsing
Andreas Vlachos and Stephen Clark

Towards README-EVAL : Interpreting README File Instructions
James White

Freebase QA: Information Extraction or Semantic Parsing?
Xuchen Yao, Jonathan Berant and Benjamin Van Durme

12:30–14:10 Lunch Break

Thursday, June 26, 2014 (continued)

Invited Talks

14:10–14:50 *Semantic Parsing for Cancer Panomics*
Hoifung Poon

14:50–15:30 *Semantics for Semantic Parsers*
Mark Steedman

15:30–16:00 Coffee Break

16:00–16:40 *Asking for Help Using Inverse Semantics*
Stefanie Tellex

16:40–17:20 *Computing with Natural Language*
Percy Liang

17:20–18:00 *Grounded Semantic Parsing*
Luke Zettlemoyer

18:00–18:00 Closing

Learning a Lexicon for Broad-Coverage Semantic Parsing

James F. Allen
Dept. of Computer Science, University of Rochester
james@cs.rochester.edu

Abstract

While there has been significant recent work on learning semantic parsers for specific task/ domains, the results don't transfer from one domain to another domains. We describe a project to learn a broad-coverage semantic lexicon for domain independent semantic parsing. The technique involves several bootstrapping steps starting from a semantic parser based on a modest-sized hand-built semantic lexicon. We demonstrate that the approach shows promise in building a semantic lexicon on the scale of WordNet, with more coverage and detail that currently available in widely-used resources such as VerbNet. We view having such a lexicon as a necessary prerequisite for any attempt at attaining broad-coverage semantic parsing in any domain. The approach we described applies to all word classes, but in this paper we focus here on verbs, which are the most critical phenomena facing semantic parsing.

1. Introduction and Motivation

Recently we have seen an explosion of work on learning semantic parsers (e.g., Matuszek, et al, 2012; Tellex et al, 2013; Branavan et al, 2010, Chen et al, 2011). While such work shows promise, the results are highly domain dependent and useful only for that domain. One cannot, for instance, reuse a lexical entry learned in one robotic domain in another robotic domain, let alone in a database query domain. Furthermore, the techniques being developed require domains that are simple enough so that the semantic models can be produced, either by hand or induced from the application. Language in general, however, involves much more complex concepts and connections, including discussion of involves abstract concepts, such as plans, theories, political views, and so on. It is not clear how the techniques currently being developed could be generalized to such language.

The challenge we are addressing is learning a broad-coverage, domain-independent semantic parser, i.e., a semantic parser that can be used in any domain. At present, there is a tradeoff between the depth of semantic representation produced and the coverage of the techniques. One of the critical gaps in enabling more general, deeper semantic systems is the lack of any broad-coverage deep semantic lexicon. Such a lexicon must contain at least the following information:

i. an enumeration of the set of distinct senses for the word (e.g., as in WordNet, PropBank), linked into an ontology that supports reasoning

ii. For each sense, we would have
- *Deep argument structure*, i.e., semantic roles with selectional preferences
- *Constructions* that map syntax to the deep argument structure (a.k.a. linking rules)
- *Lexical entailments* that characterize the temporal consequences of the event described by the verb

The closest example to such lexical entries can be found in VerbNet (Kipper et al, 2008), a hand-built resource widely used for a range of general applications. An example entry from VerbNet is seen in Figure 1, which describes a class of verbs called murder-42.1. VerbNet clusters verbs by the constructions they take, not by sense or meaning, although many times, the set of constructions a verb takes is a good feature for clustering by semantic meaning. We see that the verbs in this class can take an AGENT, PATIENT and INSTRUMENT role, and we see the possible constructions that map syntactic structure to the deep argument structure. For instance, the first entry indicates that the simple transitive construction has the AGENT as the subject and the PATIENT as the object. In addition, it specifies lexical entailments in an informal notation, roughly stating that murder verbs involve causing a event that is a transition from being alive to not being alive. Unfortunately, VerbNet only covers a few thousand verbs. This paper reports on work to automatically build entries with much greater coverage and more detail than found in VerbNet, for all the senses in WordNet. This includes the deep argument structure and constructions for each sense, as well as axioms describing lexical entailments, expressed in a formally defined

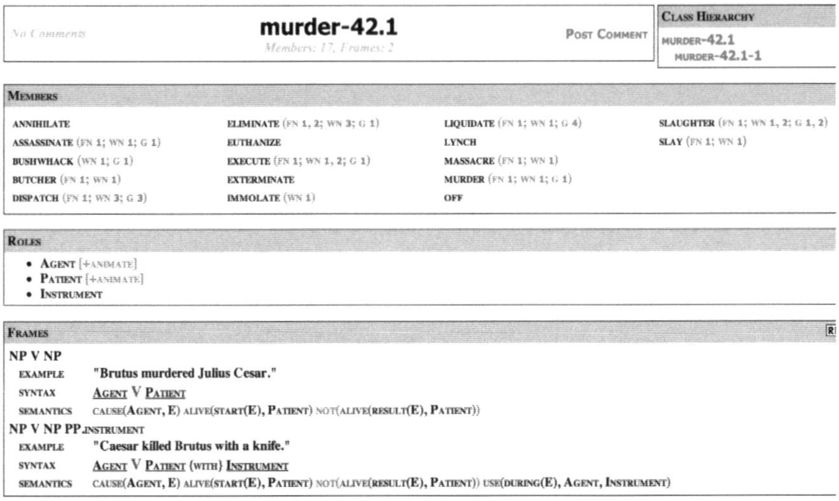

Figure 1: VerbNet Entry for murder

temporal logic (Allen, 1984; Allen & Teng, 2013).

2. Overview of the Approach

To attain broader coverage of the verbs (and their senses) for English, we look to WordNet. Though WordNet has excellent coverage, it does not contain information about argument structure, and has varying quality of ontological information (good for nouns, some information for verbs, and little for adjective and adverbs). But it does contain rich sources of information in unstructured form, i.e., each sense has a gloss that defines the word's meaning, and often provides examples of the word's usage. The technique we describe here uses an existing hand-built, but relatively limited coverage, semantic lexicon to bootstrap into a comprehensive lexicon by processing these definitions and examples. In other words, we are learning the lexicon by reading the dictionary.

Specifically, we use the TRIPS parser (Allen et al, 2008) as the starting point, which has a semantic lexicon of verbs about the same size as VerbNet. To build the comprehensive semantic lexicon, we use two bootstrapping steps. The first uses ontology mapping techniques to generate underspecified lexical entries for unknown words. This technique enables the parser to construct interpretations of sentences involving words not encoded in the core lexicon. We then use information extracted from the definitions and examples to build much more detailed and deeper lexical entries. We have run this process over the entire set of WordNet entries and provide preliminary results below evaluating the results along a number of key dimensions.

2.1. The TRIPS Parsing System

The TRIPS system is a packed-forest chart parser which builds constituents bottom-up using a best-first search strategy (Allen et al, 2008). The core grammar is a hand-built, lexicalized context-free grammar, augmented with feature structures and feature unification, and driven by a semantic lexicon and ontology. The core semantic lexicon[1] was constructed by hand and contains more than 7000 lemmas, For each word, it specifies its possible senses (i.e., its ontology type), and for each sense, its semantic roles and semantic preferences, and constructions for mapping from syntax to semantics.

The system uses variety of statistical and preprocessors to improve accuracy. These include the Stanford tools for POS tagging, named entity recognition and syntactic parsing. The parser produces and detailed logical form capturing the semantics of the sentence in a graphical notation equivalent to an unscoped, modal logic (Manshadi et al, 2012).

2.2. Level One Bootstrapping: Generating Lexical Entries Foe Unknown Words

The key idea in generating abstract lexical entries for unknown verbs builds from the same intuition the motivations underlying VerbNet -

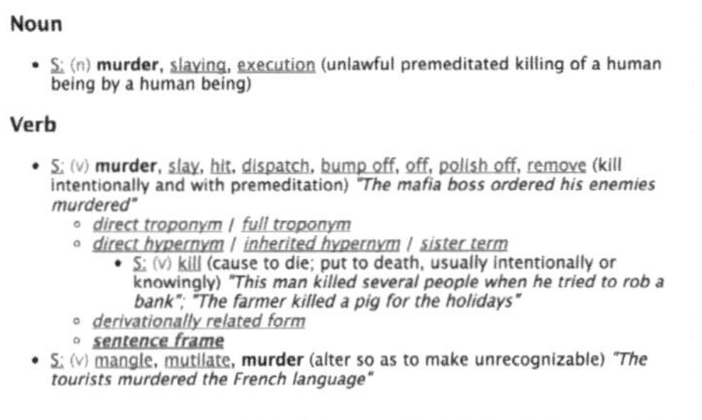

Figure 2: WordNet Entry for murder

1 you can browse the lexicon and ontology at www.cs.rochester.edu/research/trips/lexicon/browse-ont-lex.html

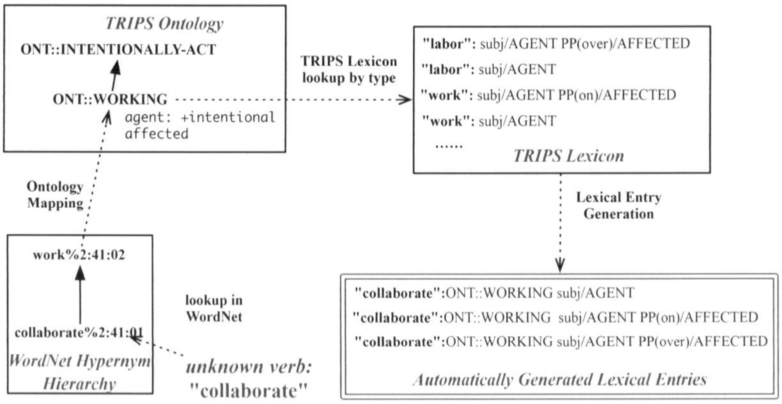

Figure 3: Example of Ontology-based Automatic Lexicon Generation

that the set of constructions a verb supports reflects its semantic meaning. While in VerbNet, the constructions are used to cluster verbs into semantic classes, we work in the opposite direction and use the semantic classes to predict the likely syntactic constructions.

To generate the lexical entries for an unknown verb we use the synset hierarchy in WordNet, plus a hand-built mapping between certain key synsets and the classes in the TRIPS ontology. The whole process operates as follows, given an unknown word *w:*

i. Look up word *w* in WordNet and obtain its possible synsets
ii. For each synset, find a mapping to the TRIPS ontology
    i. If there is a direct mapping, we are done
    ii. If not, traverse up the WordNet Hypernym hierarchy and recursively check for a mapping
iii. For each TRIPS ontology type found, gather all the words in the TRIPS lexicon that are associated with the type
iv. Take the union of all the constructions defined on the words associated with the TRIPS type
v. Generate a lexical entry for each possible combination of constructions and types

The result of this process is an over-generated set of underspecified lexical entries. Figure 3 illustrates this with a very simple example of deriving the lexical entries for the verb "collaborate": it is first looked up in WordNet, then we traverse the hypernym hierarchy until we find a mapping to the TRIPS ontology, from work%2:41:02 to ONT::WORKING. From there we find all the lexical entries associated with ONT::WORKING, and then take the union of the lexical information to produce new entries. The valid entries will be the ones that contribute to successful parses of the sentences involving the unknown words. In addition to what is shown, other lexical information is also derived in the same way, including weak selectional preferences for the argument roles.

While the result of this stage of bootstrapping produces lexical entries that identify the TRIPS type, the semantic roles and constructions, many of the lexical entries are not valid and not very deep. In particular, even considering just the correct entries, the semantic models are limited to the relatively small TRIPS ontology, and do not capture lexical entailments. Also, the selectional preferences for the semantic roles are very weak. These problems are all addressed in the second bootstrapping step.

2.3. Level Two Bootstrapping: Reading Definitions and Examples

The key idea in this stage of processing is to use the lexicon bootstrapped in level one to parse all the definitions and examples for each WordNet synset. We then use this information to build a richer ontology, better identify the semantic roles and their selectional preferences, and identify the appropriate constructions and lexical entailments. The hope is that the result is this process will be lexical entries suitable for semantic parsing, and tightly coupled with an ontology and commonsense knowledge base suitable for reasoning.

Consider an example processing a sense of the verb *keep up*, defined as *prevent from going to bed at night*. We use sense tagged glosses obtained from the Princeton Gloss Corpus to provide guidance to the parser. The TRIPS parser produces the logical form for the definition as shown in Figure 4. Each node in the graph specifies the most specific TRIPS ontology class that covers the word plus the WordNet sense. For example, the verb *prevent* is captured by a node indicating its WordNet sense prevent%2:41:00 and the TRIPS class ont::HINDERING. Note the verb *go to bed,* tagged as a multi-word verb in the Gloss corpus, has no information in the TRIPS ontology other than being an event of some sort. The semantic roles are indicated by the labelled arcs between the nodes. The nodes labelled IMPRO are the elided arguments in the definition (i.e., the missing subject and object).

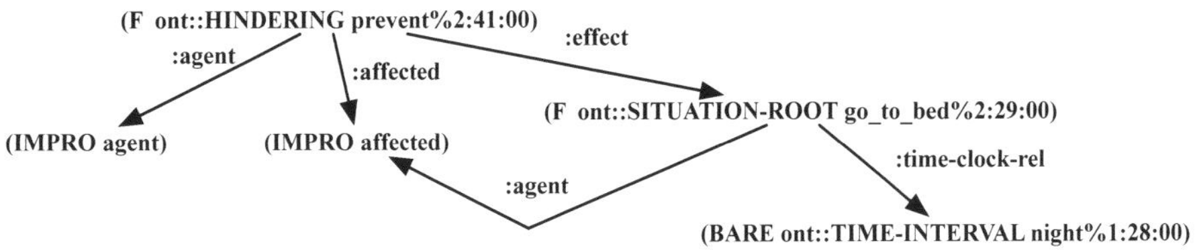

Figure 4: The parse of prevent from going to bed at night

From this definition alone we can extract several key pieces of semantic information about the verb *keep up*, namely[2]

i. Ontological: *keep_up* is a subclass of prevent %2:41:00 and ont::HINDERING events
ii. Argument Structure: *keep_up* has two semantic roles: AGENT and AFFECTED[3]
iii. Lexical Entailment: When a *keep_up* event occurs, the AGENT prevents the AFFECTED from going to bed

Definitions can be notoriously terse and complex to parse, and thus in many cases the parser can only extract key fragments of the definition. We use the TRIPS robust parsing mechanism to extract the most meaningful parse fragments when a complete parse cannot be found.

To identify the selectional preferences for the roles and the valid constructions, we parse the examples given in WordNet, plus synthetically produced sentences derived from the WordNet *sentence frame* information, plus additional examples extracted from SEMCOR, in which the words are tagged with their WordNet senses. From parsing the examples, we obtain a set of examples of the semantic roles used, plus *the constructions used to produce them.* We apply a heuristic process to combine the proposed role sets from the definitions and the glosses to arrive at a final role set for the verb. We then gather the semantic types of all the arguments from the examples, and abstract them using the derived ontology to produce the most compact set of types that cover all the examples seen. Here we present a few more details of the approach.

Determining Semantic Roles

One of the interesting observations that we discovered in this project is that the missing parts of definitions are highly predictive of the roles of the verb being defined. For instance, looking at Figure 4, we see that the verb *prevent,* used in the definition, has three roles: AGENT, AFFECTED, and EFFECT. Two of these are filled by implicit pro (**IMPRO**) forms (i.e., they were elided in the definition), and one is fully instantiated. Almost all the time it is the IMPRO roles that are promoted be the roles of *keep up*. We have found this technique to be highly reliable when we have fully accurate parsing. Because of the inevitable errors in parsing such terse language, however, we find the combining the information from the definition with additional evidence produced by parsing concrete examples gives better accuracy.

Computing Lexical Entailments

To compute lexical entailments, we use the definitions, often expanding them by recursively expanding the senses in the definition with their definitions. At some stage, the definitions of certain verb verbs become quite abstract and/or circular. To deal with this, we hand coded axiomatic definitions for a small set of aspectual verbs such as *start*, *end*, and *continue*, and causal verbs such as *cause, prevent, stop*, in a temporal logic. When a definition is expanded to the point of including one of these verbs, we can create a "temporal map" of entailments from the event. Thus, from the definition of *keep up*, we can infer that the event of going to bed does not occur over the time over which the *keep up* event occurs. A description of our first attempt to generate entailments can be found in Allen et al (2011), and the temporal logic we have developed to support compositional derivation of entailments is described in Allen & Teng (2013).

Computing Selectional Preferences

We compute selectional preferences by gathering the ontological types of elements that fill each argument position, using examples drawn from WordNet and SEMCOR. We then generalize this set by trying to find non-trivial subsuming types that cover the examples. For example, for the verb *kill*, we might find examples of the AFFECTED role of being a *person*, a *pig*, and a *plant.* We try to find a subsuming type that covers all of these classes that is more specific than the extremely abstract classes such as

---

2 The ontology is represented in OWL-DL (www.w3.org/TR/owl-guide), and the entailments in a logic based on Allen's (1984) Logic of Action and Time. There is no space to present these details in this paper.

3 The AFFECTED role in TRIPS includes most cases using the PATIENT role in VerbNet

REFERENTIAL-SEM (the class of all things that can be referred to). We compute this over a combined ontology using the TRIPS ontology plus the ontology that we derive from parsing all the WordNet definitions. Using both allows us to avoid the pitfalls of lack of coverage in one source or the other. As an example, in this case we would find the class LIVING-THING covers the three examples above, so this would be the derived selectional preference for this role of *kill*. Selectional preferences derived by the method have been shown to be useful in automatically identifying metaphors (Wilks et al, 2013).

3. Evaluations

This is a work in progress, so we do not yet have a comprehensive evaluation. We do have preliminary evaluations of specific aspects of the lexical entries we are producing, however. For the most part, our evaluations have been performed using set of human judges (some fellow colleagues and some recruited using Amazon Turk). Because of the complexity of such judging tasks, we generally use at least seven judges, and sometimes up to eleven. We then eliminate cases where there is not substantial human agreement, typically at least 75%. We have found that this eliminates less that 20% of the potential test cases. The remaining cases provide a gold standard.

The Event Ontology

To evaluate the derived event ontology, we randomly created a evaluation set consisting of 1) subclass pairs derived by our system, 2) hypernym pairs extracted from WordNet, and 3) random pairs of classes. We used eleven human judges to judge whether one class is a subclass of the other, and evaluated the system on the cases where at least eight judges in agreement (83% of cases). The system had 83% precision and 42% recall in this test, indicating good accuracy. The low recall score, however, indicates our techniques do not extract many of the hypernym relations present in WordNet. It suggests that we should also incorporate the hypernym relations as a ontology source when constructing the final deep semantic lexicon. More details can be found in Allen et al (2013).

Causal Relations Between Events

We used a similar technique to evaluate our ability to extract causal relationships between events classes (e.g., *kill* causes *die*). We tested on a similar blend of derived casual relations, explicitly annotated causal relations in WordNet and random other pairs. The system achieved 100% precision and 55% recall on this test. Interestingly, there was almost no overlap between the system-derived causal relations and those in WordNet, indicating that combining the two sources will produce a much richer resource. More details can be found in Allen et al (2013).

Selectional Preferences for Roles

We performed a preliminary evaluation on the correctness of the selectional preferences by comparing our derived classes with the restrictions in VerbNet. This is not an ideal evaluation as the VerbNet restrictions are quite abstract. For instance, VerbNet has one class for abstract objects, whereas the our derived ontology has a much richer classification, including plans, words, properties, beliefs, and so on. Thus, we expected that often our derived preferences would be more specific than the VerbNet restrictions. On a test set of 50 randomly selected verbs, 51% of the restrictions were exactly correct, 26% were too specific, 19% too general, and 2% were inconsistent. These results suggest promise for the approach. We are designing a more refined experiment using human judges to attempt to drill deeper.

4. Conclusion

The preliminary evaluations are promising and suggest it could be feasible to automatically build a deep semantic lexicon on the scale of WordNet, tightly integrated with an ontology also derived from the same sources. We are continuing this work in a number of directions, and designing better evaluation metrics. In addition, as many researchers find the WordNet inventory of word senses too fine grained, we are developing techniques that used the derived information to automatically cluster sets of senses in more abstract senses that cover them.

When the project is completed, we will be releasing the full semantic lexicon for use by other researchers.

As a final note, while the TRIPS system is an essential part of the bootstrapping process, it is trivial to remove all traces of TRIPS in the final resource, removing the hand-built lexical entries and the TRIPS ontology, leaving a resource entirely grounded in WordNet.

5. Acknowledgements

This paper summarizes work performed over a several years involving a large group of people including William de Beaumont, Hyuckchul Jung, Lucian Galescu, Janson Orfan, Mary Swift, and Choh Man Teng. This work was supported in part by NSF grant 0958193, ONR grant N000141110417, and the Nuance Foundation.

6. References

Allen, J. F. (1984). "Towards a General Theory of Action and Time." Artifical Intelligence 23: 123-154.

Allen, J., M. Swift and W. de Beaumont (2008). Deep Semantic Analysis for Text Processing. Symposium on Semantics in Systems for Text Processing (STEP 2008)

Allen, J., W. de Beaumont, et al. (2011). Acquiring Commonsense Knowledge for a Cognitive Agent. AAAI Symposium on Advances in Cognitive Systems, Washington, DC.

Allen, J., W. de Beaumont, et al. (2013). Automatically Deriving Event Ontologies for a CommonSense Knowledge Base. Proc. 10th International Conference on Computational Semantics (IWCS 2013), Potsdam, Germany.

Allen, J. and C. M. Teng (2013). Becoming Different: A Language-driven formalism for commonsense knowledge. CommonSense 2013: 11th Intl Symposium on Logical Formalization on Commonsense Reasoning, Cypress.

Branavan, S., L. Zettlemoyer, and R. Barzilay. (2010) Reading between the lines: Learning to map high-level instructions to commands. In ACL, pages 1268–1277.

Chen D.L., and R. Mooney.(2011) Learning to interpret natural language navigation instructions from observations. Proc. AAAI (AAAI-2011), pages 859–865

Dzikovska, M., J. F. Allen, et al. (2008). "Linking Semantic and Knowledge Representation in a Multi-Domain Dialogue System." Logic and Computation 18(3): 405-430.

Fellbaum, S. (1998, ed.) WordNet: An Electronic Lexical Database. Cambridge, MA: MIT Pr

Kipper, K, A Korhonen, N Ryant, M Palmer. (2008) "A Large-scale Classification of English Verbs." Language Resources and Evaluation Journal,42(1).

Manshadi, M. and J. Allen (2012a). A Universal Representation for Shallow and Deep Semantics. LREC Workshop on Semantic Annotation. Instanbul, Turkey.

Matuszek, C., E Herbst, L Zettlemoyer, D. Fox (2012), Learning to Parse Natural Language Commands to a Robot Control System, Proc. of the 13th International Symposium on Experimental Robotics (ISER)

Tellex, S., P Thaker, J Joseph, N Roy. (2013). Learning Perceptually Grounded Word Meanings From Unaligned Parallel Data. Machine Learning Journal

Wilks, Y., L. Galescu, et al. (2013). Automatic Metaphor Detection using Large-Scale Lexical Resources and Conventional Metaphor Extraction. Proceedings of the First Workshop on Metaphor in NLP, Atlanta, GA.

Semantic Parsing using Distributional Semantics and Probabilistic Logic

Islam Beltagy[§] **Katrin Erk**[†] **Raymond Mooney**[§]
[§]Department of Computer Science
[†]Department of Linguistics
The University of Texas at Austin
Austin, Texas 78712
[§]{beltagy,mooney}@cs.utexas.edu
[†]katrin.erk@mail.utexas.edu

Abstract

We propose a new approach to semantic parsing that is not constrained by a fixed formal ontology and purely logical inference. Instead, we use distributional semantics to generate only the relevant part of an on-the-fly ontology. Sentences and the on-the-fly ontology are represented in probabilistic logic. For inference, we use probabilistic logic frameworks like Markov Logic Networks (MLN) and Probabilistic Soft Logic (PSL). This semantic parsing approach is evaluated on two tasks, Textual Entitlement (RTE) and Textual Similarity (STS), both accomplished using inference in probabilistic logic. Experiments show the potential of the approach.

1 Introduction

Semantic Parsing is probably best defined as the task of representing the meaning of a natural language sentence in some formal knowledge representation language that supports automated inference. A semantic parser is best defined as having three parts, a formal language, an ontology, and an inference mechanism. Both the formal language (e.g. first-order logic) and the ontology define the formal knowledge representation. The formal language uses predicate symbols from the ontology, and the ontology provides them with meanings by defining the relations between them.[1]. A formal expression by itself without an ontology is insufficient for semantic interpretation; we call it uninterpreted logical form. An uninterpreted logical form is not enough as a knowledge representation because the predicate symbols do not have meaning in themselves, they get this meaning from the ontology. Inference is what takes a problem represented in the formal knowledge representation and the ontology and performs the target task (e.g. textual entailment, question answering, etc.).

Prior work in standard semantic parsing uses a pre-defined set of predicates in a fixed ontology. However, it is difficult to construct formal ontologies of properties and relations that have broad coverage, and very difficult to do semantic parsing based on such an ontology. Consequently, current semantic parsers are mostly restricted to fairly limited domains, such as querying a specific database (Kwiatkowski et al., 2013; Berant et al., 2013).

We propose a semantic parser that is not restricted to a predefined ontology. Instead, we use distributional semantics to generate the needed part of an *on-the-fly* ontology. Distributional semantics is a statistical technique that represents the meaning of words and phrases as distributions over context words (Turney and Pantel, 2010; Landauer and Dumais, 1997). Distributional information can be used to predict semantic relations like synonymy and hyponymy between words and phrases of interest (Lenci and Benotto, 2012; Kotlerman et al., 2010). The collection of predicted semantic relations is the "on-the-fly ontology" our semantic parser uses. A distributional semantics is relatively easy to build from a large corpus of raw text, and provides the wide coverage that formal ontologies lack.

The formal language we would like to use in the semantic parser is first-order logic. However, distributional information is graded in nature, so the on-the-fly ontology and its predicted semantic relations are also graded. This means, that standard first-order logic is insufficient because it is binary by nature. Probabilistic logic solves this problem because it accepts *weighted* first order logic formulas. For example, in probabilistic logic, the

[1]For conciseness, here we use the term "ontology" to refer to a set of predicates as well as a knowledge base (KB) of axioms that defines a complex set of relationships between them

Proceedings of the ACL 2014 Workshop on Semantic Parsing, pages 7–11,
Baltimore, Maryland USA, June 26 2014. ©2014 Association for Computational Linguistics

synonymy relation between "man" and "guy" is represented by: $\forall x.\, man(x) \Leftrightarrow guy(x) \mid w_1$ and the hyponymy relation between "car" and "vehicle" is: $\forall x.\, car(x) \Rightarrow vehicle(x) \mid w_2$ where w_1 and w_1 are some certainty measure estimated from the distributional semantics.

For inference, we use probabilistic logic frameworks like Markov Logic Networks (MLN) (Richardson and Domingos, 2006) and Probabilistic Soft Logic (PSL) (Kimmig et al., 2012). They are Statistical Relational Learning (SRL) techniques (Getoor and Taskar, 2007) that combine logical and statistical knowledge in one uniform framework, and provide a mechanism for coherent probabilistic inference. We implemented this semantic parser (Beltagy et al., 2013; Beltagy et al., 2014) and used it to perform two tasks that require deep semantic analysis, Recognizing Textual Entailment (RTE), and Semantic Textual Similarity (STS).

The rest of the paper is organized as follows: section 2 presents background material, section 3 explains the three components of the semantic parser, section 4 shows how this semantic parser can be used for RTE and STS tasks, section 5 presents the evaluation and 6 concludes.

2 Background

2.1 Logical Semantics

Logic-based representations of meaning have a long tradition (Montague, 1970; Kamp and Reyle, 1993). They handle many complex semantic phenomena such as relational propositions, logical operators, and quantifiers; however, they can not handle "graded" aspects of meaning in language because they are binary by nature. Also, the logical predicates and relations do not have semantics by themselves without an accompanying ontology, which we want to replace in our semantic parser with distributional semantics.

To map a sentence to logical form, we use Boxer (Bos, 2008), a tool for wide-coverage semantic analysis that produces uninterpreted logical forms using Discourse Representation Structures (Kamp and Reyle, 1993). It builds on the C&C CCG parser (Clark and Curran, 2004).

2.2 Distributional Semantics

Distributional models use statistics on contextual data from large corpora to predict semantic similarity of words and phrases (Turney and Pantel, 2010; Mitchell and Lapata, 2010), based on the observation that semantically similar words occur in similar contexts (Landauer and Dumais, 1997; Lund and Burgess, 1996). So words can be represented as vectors in high dimensional spaces generated from the contexts in which they occur. Distributional models capture the graded nature of meaning, but do not adequately capture logical structure (Grefenstette, 2013). It is possible to compute vector representations for larger phrases compositionally from their parts (Landauer and Dumais, 1997; Mitchell and Lapata, 2008; Mitchell and Lapata, 2010; Baroni and Zamparelli, 2010; Grefenstette and Sadrzadeh, 2011). Distributional similarity is usually a mixture of semantic relations, but particular *asymmetric* similarity measures can, to a certain extent, predict hypernymy and lexical entailment distributionally (Lenci and Benotto, 2012; Kotlerman et al., 2010).

2.3 Markov Logic Network

Markov Logic Network (MLN) (Richardson and Domingos, 2006) is a framework for probabilistic logic that employ weighted formulas in first-order logic to compactly encode complex undirected probabilistic graphical models (i.e., Markov networks). Weighting the rules is a way of softening them compared to hard logical constraints. MLNs define a probability distribution over possible worlds, where a world's probability increases exponentially with the total weight of the logical clauses that it satisfies. A variety of inference methods for MLNs have been developed, however, their computational complexity is a fundamental issue.

2.4 Probabilistic Soft Logic

Probabilistic Soft Logic (PSL) is another recently proposed framework for probabilistic logic (Kimmig et al., 2012). It uses logical representations to compactly define large graphical models with continuous variables, and includes methods for performing efficient probabilistic inference for the resulting models. A key distinguishing feature of PSL is that ground atoms have soft, continuous truth values in the interval [0, 1] rather than binary truth values as used in MLNs and most other probabilistic logics. Given a set of weighted inference rules, and with the help of Lukasiewicz's relaxation of the logical operators, PSL builds a graphical model defining a probability distribution over the continuous space of values of the random variables in the model. Then, PSL's MPE inference (Most Probable Explanation) finds the overall interpretation with the maximum probability given a set of evidence. It turns out that this optimization problem is second-order cone program (SOCP) (Kimmig et al., 2012) and can be solved efficiently in polynomial time.

2.5 Recognizing Textual Entailment

Recognizing Textual Entailment (RTE) is the task of determining whether one natural language text, the *premise*, Entails, Contradicts, or not related (Neutral) to another, the *hypothesis*.

2.6 Semantic Textual Similarity

Semantic Textual Similarity (STS) is the task of judging the similarity of a pair of sentences on a scale from 1 to 5 (Agirre et al., 2012). Gold standard scores are averaged over multiple human annotations and systems are evaluated using the Pearson correlation between a system's output and gold standard scores.

3 Approach

A semantic parser is three components, a formal language, an ontology, and an inference mechanism. This section explains the details of these components in our semantic parser. It also points out the future work related to each part of the system.

3.1 Formal Language: first-order logic

Natural sentences are mapped to logical form using Boxer (Bos, 2008), which maps the input sentences into a lexically-based logical form, in which the predicates are words in the sentence. For example, the sentence "A man is driving a car" in logical form is:

$\exists x, y, z.\ man(x) \land agent(y, x) \land drive(y) \land patient(y, z) \land car(z)$

We call Boxer's output alone an uninterpreted logical form because predicates do not have meaning by themselves. They still need to be connected with an ontology.

Future work: While Boxer has wide coverage, additional linguistic phenomena like generalized quantifiers need to be handled.

3.2 Ontology: on-the-fly ontology

Distributional information is used to generate the needed part of an on-the-fly ontology for the given input sentences. It is encoded in the form of weighted inference rules describing the semantic relations connecting words and phrases in the input sentences. For example, for sentences "A man is driving a car", and "A guy is driving a vehicle", we would like to generate rules like $\forall x.\ man(x) \Leftrightarrow guy(x) \mid w_1$ indicating that "man" and "guy" are synonyms with some certainty w_1, and $\forall x.\ car(x) \Rightarrow vehicle(x) \mid w_2$ indicating that "car" is a hyponym of "vehicle" with some certainty w_2. Other semantic relations can also be easily encoded as inference rules like antonyms $\forall x.\ tall(x) \Leftrightarrow \neg short(x) \mid w$, contextonymy relation $\forall x.\ hospital(x) \Rightarrow \exists y.\ doctor(y) \mid w$. For now, we generate inference rules only as synonyms (Beltagy et al., 2013), but we are experimenting with more types of semantic relations.

In (Beltagy et al., 2013), we generate inference rules between all pairs of words and phrases. Given two input sentences T and H, for all pairs (a, b), where a and b are words or phrases of T and H respectively, generate an inference rule: $a \rightarrow b \mid w$, where the rule's weight $w = sim(\overrightarrow{a}, \overrightarrow{b})$, and sim is the $cosine$ of the angle between vectors $\overrightarrow{a}$ and $\overrightarrow{b}$. Note that this similarity measure cannot yet distinguish relations like synonymy and hypernymy. Phrases are defined in terms of Boxer's output to be more than one unary atom sharing the same variable like "a little kid" which in logic is $little(k) \land kid(k)$, or two unary atoms connected by a relation like "a man is driving" which in logic is $man(m) \land agent(d, m) \land drive(d)$. We used vector addition (Mitchell and Lapata, 2010) to calculate vectors for phrases.

Future Work: This can be extended in many directions. We are currently experimenting with asymmetric similarity functions to distinguish semantic relations. We would also like to use longer phrases and other compositionality techniques as in (Baroni and Zamparelli, 2010; Grefenstette and Sadrzadeh, 2011). Also more inference rules can be added from paraphrases collections like PPDB (Ganitkevitch et al., 2013).

3.3 Inference: probabilistic logical inference

The last component is probabilistic logical inference. Given the logical form of the input sentences, and the weighted inference rules, we use them to build a probabilistic logic program whose solution is the answer to the target task. A probabilistic logic program consists of the evidence set

E, the set of weighted first order logical expressions (rule base RB), and a query Q. Inference is the process of calculating $Pr(Q|E, RB)$.

Probabilistic logic frameworks define a probability distribution over all possible worlds. The number of constants in a world depends on the number of the discourse entities in the Boxer output, plus additional constants introduced to handle quantification. Mostly, all constants are combined with all literals, except for rudimentary type checking.

4 Tasks

This section explains how we perform the RTE and STS tasks using our semantic parser.

4.1 Task 1: RTE using MLNs

MLNs are the probabilistic logic framework we use for the RTE task (we do not use PSL here as it shares the problems of fuzzy logic with probabilistic reasoning). The RTE's classification problem for the relation between T and H, and given the rule base RB generated as in 3.2, can be split into two inference tasks. The first is finding if T entails H, $Pr(H|T, RB)$. The second is finding if the negation of the text $\neg T$ entails H, $Pr(H|\neg T, RB)$. In case $Pr(H|T, RB)$ is high, while $Pr(H|\neg T, RB)$ is low, this indicates Entails. In case it is the other way around, this indicates Contradicts. If both values are close to each other, this means T does not affect probability of H and that is an indication of Neutral. We train a classifier to map the two values to the final classification decision.

Future Work: One general problem with MLNs is its computational overhead especially for the type of inference problems we have. The other problem is that MLNs, as with most other probabilistic logics, make the Domain Closure Assumption (Richardson and Domingos, 2006) which means that quantifiers sometimes behave in an undesired way.

4.2 Task 2: STS using PSL

PSL is the probabilistic logic we use for the STS task since it has been shown to be an effective approach to compute similarity between structured objects. PSL does not work "out of the box" for STS, because Lukasiewicz's equation for the conjunction is very restrictive. We addressed this problem (Beltagy et al., 2014) by replacing Lukasiewicz's equation for the conjunction with an averaging equation, then change the optimization problem and the grounding technique accordingly.

	SICK-RTE	SICK-STS
dist	0.60	0.65
logic	0.71	0.68
logic+dist	0.73	0.70

Table 1: RTE accuracy and STS Correlation

For each STS pair of sentences S_1, S_2, we run PSL twice, once where $E = S_1$, $Q = S_2$ and another where $E = S_2$, $Q = S_1$, and output the two scores. The final similarity score is produced from a regressor trained to map the two PSL scores to the overall similarity score.

Future Work: Use a weighted average where different weights are learned for different parts of the sentence.

5 Evaluation

The dataset used for evaluation is **SICK**: Sentences Involving Compositional Knowledge dataset, a task for SemEval 2014. The initial data release for the competition consists of 5,000 pairs of sentences which are annotated for both RTE and STS. For this evaluation, we performed 10-fold cross validation on this initial data.

Table 1 shows results comparing our full approach (**logic+dist**) to two baselines, a distributional-only baseline (**dist**) that uses vector addition, and a probabilistic logic-only baseline (**logic**) which is our semantic parser without distributional inference rules. The integrated approach (**logic+dist**) out-performs both baselines.

6 Conclusion

We presented an approach to semantic parsing that has a wide-coverage for words and relations, and does not require a fixed formal ontology. An on-the-fly ontology of semantic relations between predicates is derived from distributional information and encoded in the form of soft inference rules in probabilistic logic. We evaluated this approach on two task, RTE and STS, using two probabilistic logics, MLNs and PSL respectively. The semantic parser can be extended in different direction, especially in predicting more complex semantic relations, and enhancing the inference mechanisms.

Acknowledgments

This research was supported by the DARPA DEFT program under AFRL grant FA8750-13-2-0026. Any opinions, findings, and conclusions or recommendations expressed in this material are those of the author and do not necessarily reflect the view of DARPA, DoD or the US government. Some experiments were run on the Mastodon Cluster supported by NSF Grant EIA-0303609.

References

Eneko Agirre, Daniel Cer, Mona Diab, and Aitor Gonzalez-Agirre. 2012. Semeval-2012 task 6: A pilot on semantic textual similarity. In *Proceedings of Semantic Evaluation (SemEval-12)*.

Marco Baroni and Roberto Zamparelli. 2010. Nouns are vectors, adjectives are matrices: Representing adjective-noun constructions in semantic space. In *Proceedings of Conference on Empirical Methods in Natural Language Processing (EMNLP-10)*.

Islam Beltagy, Cuong Chau, Gemma Boleda, Dan Garrette, Katrin Erk, and Raymond Mooney. 2013. Montague meets Markov: Deep semantics with probabilistic logical form. In *Proceedings of the Second Joint Conference on Lexical and Computational Semantics (*SEM-13)*.

Islam Beltagy, Katrin Erk, and Raymond Mooney. 2014. Probabilistic soft logic for semantic textual similarity. In *Proceedings of Association for Computational Linguistics (ACL-14)*.

Jonathan Berant, Andrew Chou, Roy Frostig, and Percy Liang. 2013. Semantic parsing on Freebase from question-answer pairs. In *Proceedings of Conference on Empirical Methods in Natural Language Processing (EMNLP-13)*.

Johan Bos. 2008. Wide-coverage semantic analysis with Boxer. In *Proceedings of Semantics in Text Processing (STEP-08)*.

Stephen Clark and James R. Curran. 2004. Parsing the WSJ using CCG and log-linear models. In *Proceedings of Association for Computational Linguistics (ACL-04)*.

Juri Ganitkevitch, Benjamin Van Durme, and Chris Callison-Burch. 2013. PPDB: The paraphrase database. In *Proceedings of North American Chapter of the Association for Computational Linguistics: Human Language Technologies (NAACL-HLT-13)*.

L. Getoor and B. Taskar, editors. 2007. *Introduction to Statistical Relational Learning*. MIT Press, Cambridge, MA.

Edward Grefenstette and Mehrnoosh Sadrzadeh. 2011. Experimental support for a categorical compositional distributional model of meaning. In *Proceedings of Conference on Empirical Methods in Natural Language Processing (EMNLP-11)*.

Edward Grefenstette. 2013. Towards a formal distributional semantics: Simulating logical calculi with tensors. In *Proceedings of Second Joint Conference on Lexical and Computational Semantics (*SEM 2013)*.

Hans Kamp and Uwe Reyle. 1993. *From Discourse to Logic*. Kluwer.

Angelika Kimmig, Stephen H. Bach, Matthias Broecheler, Bert Huang, and Lise Getoor. 2012. A short introduction to Probabilistic Soft Logic. In *Proceedings of NIPS Workshop on Probabilistic Programming: Foundations and Applications (NIPS Workshop-12)*.

Lili Kotlerman, Ido Dagan, Idan Szpektor, and Maayan Zhitomirsky-Geffet. 2010. Directional distributional similarity for lexical inference. *Natural Language Engineering*.

Tom Kwiatkowski, Eunsol Choi, Yoav Artzi, and Luke Zettlemoyer. 2013. Scaling semantic parsers with on-the-fly ontology matching. In *Proceedings of Conference on Empirical Methods in Natural Language Processing (EMNLP-13)*.

T. K. Landauer and S. T. Dumais. 1997. A solution to Plato's problem: The Latent Semantic Analysis theory of the acquisition, induction, and representation of knowledge. *Psychological Review*.

Alessandro Lenci and Giulia Benotto. 2012. Identifying hypernyms in distributional semantic spaces. In *Proceedings of the first Joint Conference on Lexical and Computational Semantics (*SEM-12)*.

Kevin Lund and Curt Burgess. 1996. Producing high-dimensional semantic spaces from lexical cooccurrence. *Behavior Research Methods, Instruments, and Computers*.

Jeff Mitchell and Mirella Lapata. 2008. Vector-based models of semantic composition. In *Proceedings of Association for Computational Linguistics (ACL-08)*.

Jeff Mitchell and Mirella Lapata. 2010. Composition in distributional models of semantics. *Journal of Cognitive Science*.

Richard Montague. 1970. Universal grammar. *Theoria*, 36:373–398.

Matthew Richardson and Pedro Domingos. 2006. Markov logic networks. *Machine Learning*, 62:107–136.

Peter Turney and Patrick Pantel. 2010. From frequency to meaning: Vector space models of semantics. *Journal of Artificial Intelligence Research (JAIR-10)*.

Large-scale CCG Induction from the Groningen Meaning Bank

Sebastian Beschke[*], **Yang Liu**[†] and **Wolfgang Menzel**[*]
[*]Department of Informatics, University of Hamburg, Germany
{beschke,menzel}@informatik.uni-hamburg.de
[†]State Key Laboratory of Intelligent Technology and Systems
Tsinghua National Laboratory for Information Science and Technology
Department of Computer Science and Technology, Tsinghua University, Beijing, China
liuyang2011@tsinghua.edu.cn

Abstract

In present CCG-based semantic parsing systems, the extraction of a semantic grammar from sentence-meaning examples poses a computational challenge. An important factor is the decomposition of the sentence meaning into smaller parts, each corresponding to the meaning of a word or phrase. This has so far limited supervised semantic parsing to small, specialised corpora. We propose a set of heuristics that render the splitting of meaning representations feasible on a large-scale corpus, and present a method for grammar induction capable of extracting a semantic CCG from the Groningen Meaning Bank.

1 Introduction

Combinatory Categorial Grammar (CCG) forms the basis of many current approaches to semantic parsing. It is attractive for semantic parsing due to its unified treatment of syntax and semantics, where the construction of the meaning representation directly follows the syntactic analysis (Steedman, 2001). However, the supervised induction of semantic CCGs—the inference of a CCG from a corpus of sentence-meaning pairs—has so far only been partially solved. While approaches are available that work on small corpora focused on specific domains (such as Geoquery and Freebase QA for question answering (Zelle and Mooney, 1996; Cai and Yates, 2013)), we are not aware of any approach that allows the extraction of a semantic CCG from a wide-coverage corpus such as the Groningen Meaning Bank (GMB) (Basile et al., 2012). This work attempts to fill this gap.

Analogous to the work of Kwiatkowski et al. (2010), we view grammar induction as a series of splitting steps, each of which essentially reverses a CCG derivation step. However, we diverge from their approach by applying novel heuristics for searching the space of possible splits. The combination of alignment consistency and single-branching recursion turns out to produce a manageable number of lexical items for most sentences in the GMB, while statistical measures and manual inspection suggest that many of these items are also plausible.

2 Searching the space of CCG derivations

Our search heuristics are embedded into a very general splitting algorithm, Algorithm 1. Given a sentence-meaning pair, it iterates over all possible sentence-meaning splits in two steps. First, a split index in the sentence is chosen along with a binary CCG-combinator to be reversed (the *syntactic split*). Then, the meaning representation is split accordingly to reverse the application of the selected combinator (the *semantic split*). E. g., for the forward application combinator, the meaning representation z is split into f, g so that $z = fg$ (modulo α, β, η conversions). By identifying f with the left half l of the sentence and g with the right half r, we obtain two new phrase-meaning pairs, which are then split recursively.

This algorithm combines two challenging search problems. Recursive syntactic splitting searches the space of syntactic CCG derivations that yield the sentence, which is exponential in the length of the sentence. Semantic splitting, given the flexibility of λ-calculus, has infinitely many solutions. The crucial question is how to prune the parts of the search space that are unlikely to lead to good results.

Our strategy to address this problem is to apply heuristics that constrain the results returned by semantic splitting. By yielding no results on certain inputs, this at the same time constrains the syntactic search space. The following descriptions there-

Proceedings of the ACL 2014 Workshop on Semantic Parsing, pages 12–16,
Baltimore, Maryland USA, June 26 2014.

fore relate to the implementation of the SEMSPLIT function.

Algorithm 1 A general splitting algorithm. $\mathcal{C}$ is the set of binary CCG combinators. The SEMSPLIT function returns possible splits of a meaning representation according to the reverse application of a combinator.

function SPLIT(x, z)
    if $|x| = 1$ **then**
        return $\{(x, z)\}$
    else
        $G \leftarrow \emptyset$
        for $0 < i \leq |x| - 1$ and $c \in \mathcal{C}$ **do**
            $l \leftarrow x_0 \ldots x_{i-1}$
            $r \leftarrow x_i \ldots x_{|x|-1}$
            $S \leftarrow$ SEMSPLIT(c, z)
            for $(f, g) \in S$ **do**
                $G \leftarrow G \cup$ SPLIT(l, f)
                        $\cup$ SPLIT(r, g)
            end for
        end for
        return G
    end if
end function

2.1 Alignment consistency

The first heuristic we introduce is borrowed from the field of statistical machine translation. There, alignments between words of two languages are used to identify corresponding phrase pairs, as in the well-known GHKM algorithm (Galley et al., 2004). In order to apply the same strategy to meaning representations, we represent them as their abstract syntax trees. Following Li et al. (2013), we can then align words in the sentence and nodes in the meaning representation to identify components that correspond to each other.

This allows us to impose an extra constraint on the generation of splits: We require that nodes in f not be aligned to any words in the right sentence-half r, and conversely, that nodes in g not be aligned to words in l.

Alignment consistency helps the search to focus on more plausible splits by grouping elements of the meaning representation with the words that evoked them. However, by itself it does not significantly limit the search space, as it is still possible to extract infinitely many semantic splits from any sentence at any splitting index.

Example: Given the word-to-meaning

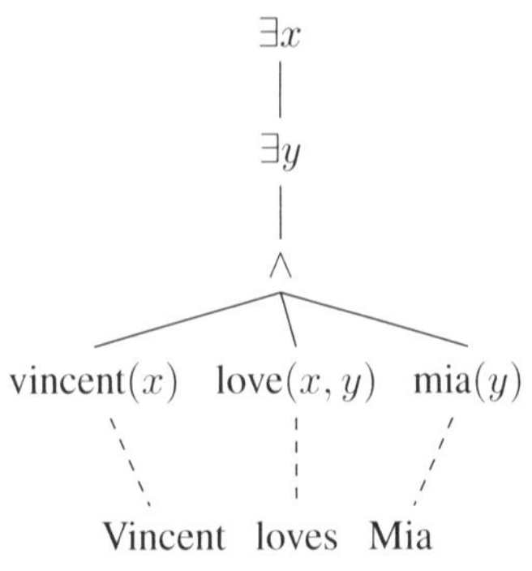

Figure 1: An example word-to-meaning alignment. Splits across any of the alignment edges are prohibited. E. g., we cannot produce a split whose meaning representation contains both vincent and mia.

alignment from Figure 1, a split that is excluded by the alignment criterion is: (Vincent : $\lambda g.\exists x.\exists y.\text{vincent}(x) \wedge \text{love}(x, y) \wedge g(y)$), (loves Mia : $\lambda y.\text{mia}(y)$). This is because the node "love" (in f) is aligned to the word "loves" (in r).

2.2 Single-branching recursive splitting

The second heuristic is best described as a search strategy over possible semantic splits. In the following presentation, we presume that alignment consistency is being enforced. Again, it is helpful to view the meaning representation as an abstract syntax tree.

Recall that our goal is to find two expressions f, g to be associated with the sentence halves l, r. In a special case, this problem is easily solved: If we can find some *split node* X which governs all nodes aligned to words in r, but no nodes aligned to words in l, we can simply extract the sub-tree rooted at X and replace it with a variable. E. g., $z = a(bc)$ can be split into $f = \lambda x.a(xc)$ and $g = b$, which can be recombined by application.

However, requiring the existence of exactly two such contiguous components can be overly restrictive, as Figure 2 illustrates. Instead, we say that we decompose z into a hierarchy of components, with a split node at the root of each component. These components are labelled as f- and g-components in an alternating fashion.

In this hierarchy, the members of an f-component are not allowed to have alignments to words in l. A corresponding requirement holds for

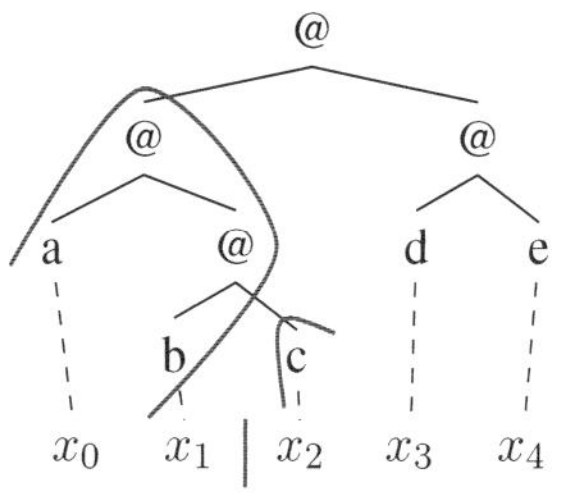

Figure 2: Illustration of single-branching recursion: Assume that the leaves of the meaning representation $a(bc)(de)$ are aligned as given to the words $x_0 \dots x_4$, and that we wish to split the sentence at index 2. The indicated split partitions the meaning representation into three hierarchically nested components and yields $f = \lambda x.xc(de)$ and $g = \lambda y.a(by)$, which can be recombined using application.

g-components.

The *single-branching* criterion states that all split nodes lie on a common path from the root, or in other words, every component is the parent of at most one sub-component.

In comparison to more flexible strategies, single-branching recursive splitting has the advantage of requiring a minimum of additionally generated structure. For every component, we only need to introduce one new bound variable for the body plus one for every variable that occurs free under the split node.

Together with the alignment consistency criterion, single-branching recursive splitting limits the search space sufficiently to make a full search tractable in many cases.

2.3 Other heuristics

The following heuristics seem promising but are left to be explored in future work.

Min-cut splitting In this strategy, we place no restriction on which split nodes are chosen. Instead, we require that the overall count of split nodes is minimal, which is equivalent to saying that the edges cut by the split form a minimum cut separating the nodes aligned to the left and right halves of the sentence, respectively. This strategy has the advantage of being able to handle any alignment/split point combination, but requires a more complex splitting pattern and thus more additional structure than single-branching recursion.

Syntax-driven splitting Since CCG is based on the assumption that semantic and syntactic derivations are isomorphic, we might use syntactic annotations to guide the search of the derivation space and only consider splits along constituent boundaries. Syntactic annotations might be present in the data or generated by standard tools. However, initial tests have shown that this requirement is too restrictive when combined with our two main heuristics.

Obviously, an effective combination of heuristics needs to be found. One particular configuration which seems promising is alignment consistency combined with min-cut splitting (which is more permissive than single-branching recursion) and syntax-driven splitting (which adds an extra restriction).

3 Discussion

We present some empirical observations about the behaviour of the above-mentioned heuristics. Our observations are based on a grammar extracted from the GMB. A formal evaluation of our system in the context of a full semantic parsing system is left for future work.

3.1 Implementation

Currently, our system implements single-branching recursive splitting along with alignment consistency. We extracted the word-to-meaning alignments from the CCG derivations annotated in the GMB, but kept only alignment edges to predicate nodes. Sentence grammars were extracted by generating an initial item for each sentence and feeding it to the SPLIT procedure.

In addition to alignment consistency and single-branching recursion, we enforce three simple criteria to rule out highly implausible items: The count of arrows in an extracted meaning representation's type is limited to eight, the number of split nodes is limited to three, and the number of free variables in extracted components is also limited to three.

A major limitation of our implementation is that it currently only considers the application combinator during splitting. We take this as a main reason for the limited granularity we observe in our output. Generalisation of the splitting implementation to other combinators such as composition is therefore necessary before performing any serious evaluation.

3.2 Manual inspection

Manual inspection of the generated grammars leads to two general observations.

Firstly, many single-word items present in the CCG annotations of the GMB are recovered. While this behaviour is not required, it is encouraging, as these items exhibit a relatively simple structure and would be expected to generalise well.

At the same time, many multi-word phrases remain in the data that cannot be split further, and are therefore unlikely to generalise well. We have identified two likely causes for this phenomenon: The missing implementation of a composition combinator, and coarse alignments.

Composition splits would enable the splitting of items which do not decompose well (i. e., do not pass the search heuristics in use) under the application combinator. Since composition occurs frequently in GMB derivations, it is to be expected that its lack noticeably impoverishes the quality of the extracted grammar.

The extraction of alignments currently in use in our implementation works by retracing the CCG derivations annotated in the GMB, and thus establishing a link between a word and the set of meaning representation elements introduced by it. However, our current implementation only handles the most common derivation nodes and otherwise cuts this retracing process short, making alignments to the entire phrase governed by an intermediate node. This may cause the corresponding part of the search to be pruned due to a search space explosion. We plan to investigate using a statistical alignment tool instead, possibly using supplementary heuristics for determining aligned words and nodes. As an additional advantage, this would remove the need for annotated CCG derivations in the data.

3.3 Statistical observations

From the total 47 230 sentences present in the GMB, our software was able to extract a sentence grammar for 43 046 sentences. Failures occurred either because processing took longer than 20 minutes, because the count of items extracted for a single sentence surpassed 10 000, or due to processing errors.

On average, 825 items were extracted per sentence with a median of 268. After removing duplicate items, the combined grammar for the whole GMB consisted of about 32 million items. While the running time of splitting is still exponential and gets out of hand on some examples, most sentences are processed within seconds.

Single-word items were extracted for 46% of word occurrences. Ideally, we would like to obtain single-word items for as many words as possible, as those items have the highest potential to generalise to unseen data. For those occurrences where no single-word item was extracted, the median length of the smallest extracted item was 12, with a maximum of 49.

4 Conclusion

We have presented a method for bringing the induction of semantic CCGs to a larger scale than has been feasible so far. Using the heuristics of alignment consistency and single-branching recursive splitting, we are able to extract a grammar from the full GMB. Our observations suggest a mixed outcome: We obtain desirable single-word items for only about half of all word occurrences. However, due to the incompleteness of the implementation and the lack of a formal evaluation, these observations do not yet permit any conclusions. In future work, we will address both of these shortcomings.

5 Final remarks

The software implementing the presented functionality is available for download[1].

This work has been supported by the German Research Foundation (DFG) as part of the CINACS international graduate research group.

References

Valerio Basile, Johan Bos, Kilian Evang, and Noortje Venhuizen. 2012. Developing a large semantically annotated corpus. In *Proceedings of LREC'12*, Istanbul, Turkey.

Qingqing Cai and Alexander Yates. 2013. Large-scale semantic parsing via schema matching and lexicon extension. In *Proceedings of ACL 2013*, Sofia, Bulgaria.

Michel Galley, Mark Hopkins, Kevin Knight, and Daniel Marcu. 2004. What's in a translation rule? In *Proceedings of HLT-NAACL 2004*, Boston, Massachusetts, USA.

[1] `http://nats-www.informatik.uni-hamburg.de/User/SebastianBeschke`

Tom Kwiatkowski, Luke Zettlemoyer, Sharon Goldwater, and Mark Steedman. 2010. Inducing probabilistic CCG grammars from logical form with higher-order unification. In *Proceedings of EMNLP 2010*, Cambridge, Massachusetts, USA.

Peng Li, Yang Liu, and Maosong Sun. 2013. An extended GHKM algorithm for inducing λ-scfg. In *Proceedings of AAAI 2013*, Bellevue, Washington, USA.

Mark Steedman. 2001. *The Syntactic Process*. MIT Press, January.

John M. Zelle and Raymond J. Mooney. 1996. Learning to parse database queries using inductive logic programming. In *Proceedings of AAAI-96*, Portland, Oregon, USA.

Semantic Parsing for Text to 3D Scene Generation

Angel X. Chang, Manolis Savva and **Christopher D. Manning**
Computer Science Department, Stanford University
angelx,msavva,manning@cs.stanford.edu

Figure 1: Generated scene for "There is a room with a chair and a computer." Note that the system infers the presence of a desk and that the computer should be supported by the desk.

1 Introduction

We propose text-to-scene generation as an application for semantic parsing. This is an application that grounds semantics in a virtual world that requires understanding of common, everyday language. In text to scene generation, the user provides a textual description and the system generates a 3D scene. For example, Figure 1 shows the generated scene for the input text "there is a room with a chair and a computer". This is a challenging, open-ended problem that prior work has only addressed in a limited way.

Most of the technical challenges in text to scene generation stem from the difficulty of mapping language to formal representations of visual scenes, as well as an overall absence of real world spatial knowledge from current NLP systems. These issues are partly due to the omission in natural language of many facts about the world. When people describe scenes in text, they typically specify only important, relevant information. Many common sense facts are unstated (e.g., chairs and desks are typically on the floor). Therefore, we focus on inferring implicit relations that are likely to hold even if they are not explicitly stated by the input text.

Text to scene generation offers a rich, interactive environment for grounded language that is familiar to everyone. The entities are common, everyday objects, and the knowledge necessary to address this problem is of general use across many domains. We present a system that leverages user interaction with 3D scenes to generate training data for semantic parsing approaches.

Previous semantic parsing work has dealt with grounding text to physical attributes and relations (Matuszek et al., 2012; Krishnamurthy and Kollar, 2013), generating text for referring to objects (FitzGerald et al., 2013) and with connecting language to spatial relationships (Golland et al., 2010; Artzi and Zettlemoyer, 2013). Semantic parsing methods can also be applied to many aspects of text to scene generation. Furthermore, work on parsing instructions to robots (Matuszek et al., 2013; Tellex et al., 2014) has analogues in the context of discourse about physical scenes.

In this extended abstract, we formalize the text to scene generation problem and describe it as a task for semantic parsing methods. To motivate this problem, we present a prototype system that incorporates simple spatial knowledge, and parses natural text to a semantic representation. By learning priors on spatial knowledge (e.g., typical positions of objects, and common spatial relations) our system addresses inference of implicit spatial constraints. The user can interactively manipulate the generated scene with textual commands, enabling us to refine and expand learned priors.

Our current system uses deterministic rules to map text to a scene representation but we plan to explore training a semantic parser from data. We can leverage our system to collect user interactions for training data. Crowdsourcing is a promising avenue for obtaining a large scale dataset.

Proceedings of the ACL 2014 Workshop on Semantic Parsing, pages 17–21,
Baltimore, Maryland USA, June 26 2014.

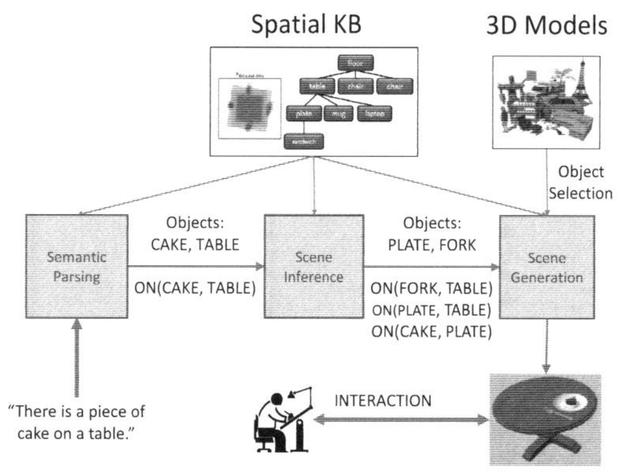

Figure 2: Illustration of our system architecture.

2 Task Definition

We define text to scene generation as the task of taking text describing a scene as input, and generating a plausible 3D scene described by that text as output. More concretely, we parse the input text into a *scene template*, which places constraints on what objects must be present and relationships between them. Next, using priors from a spatial knowledge base, the system expands the scene template by inferring additional implicit constraints. Based on the scene template, we select objects from a dataset of 3D models and arrange them to generate an output scene.

After a scene is generated, the user can interact with the scene using both textual commands and mouse interactions. During interaction, semantic parsing can be used to parse the input text into a sequence of *scene interaction commands*. See Figure 2 for an illustration of the system architecture. Throughout the process, we need to address grounding of language to: 1) actions to be performed, 2) objects to be instantiated or manipulated, and 3) constraints on the objects.

2.1 Scene Template

A scene template $\mathcal{T} = (\mathcal{O}, \mathcal{C})$ consists of a set of object descriptions $\mathcal{O} = \{o_1, \ldots, o_n\}$ and constraints $\mathcal{C} = \{c_1, \ldots, c_k\}$ on the relationships between the objects. For each object o_i, we identify properties associated with it such as category label, basic attributes such as color and material, and number of occurrences in the scene. Based on the object category and attributes, and other words in the noun phrase mentioning the object, we identify a set of associated keywords to be used later for querying the 3D model database. Spatial relations between objects are extracted as predicates of the form $on(o_i, o_j)$ or $left(o_i, o_j)$ where o_i and o_j are recognized objects.

As an example, given the input "*There is a room with a desk and a red chair. The chair is to the left of the desk.*" we extract the following objects and spatial relations:

Objects	category	attributes	keywords
o_0	room		room
o_1	desk		desk
o_2	chair	*color*:red	chair, red

Relations: $left(o_2, o_1)$

2.2 Scene Interaction Commands

During interaction, we parse textual input provided by the user into a sequence of commands with relevant parts of the scene as arguments. For example, given a scene $\mathcal{S}$, we use the input text to identify a subset of relevant objects matching $X = \{\mathcal{O}_s, \mathcal{C}_s\}$ where $\mathcal{O}_s$ is the set of object descriptions and $\mathcal{C}_s$ is the set of object constraints. Commands can then be resolved against this argument to manipulate the scene state: $Select(X)$, $Remove(X)$, $Insert(X)$, $Replace(X, Y)$, $Move(X, \Delta X)$, $Scale(X, \Delta X)$, and $Orient(X, \Delta X)$. X and Y are semantic representations of objects, while ΔX is a change to be applied to X, expressed as either a target condition ("put the lamp on the table") or a relative change ("move the lamp to the right").

These basic operations demonstrate possible scene manipulations through text. This set of operations can be enlarged to cover manipulation of parts of objects ("make the seat of the chair red"), and of the viewpoint ("zoom in on the chair").

2.3 Spatial Knowledge

One of the richest sources of spatial knowledge is 3D scene data. Prior work by (Fisher et al., 2012) collected 133 small indoor scenes created with 1723 3D Warehouse models. Based on their approach, we create a spatial knowledge base with priors on the static support hierarchy of objects in scenes[1], their relative positions and orientations. We also define a set of spatial relations such as *left, right, above, below, front, back, on top of, next to, near, inside, and outside*. Table 1 gives examples of the definitions of these spatial relations.

We use a 3D model dataset collected from Google 3D Warehouse by prior work in scene syn-

[1] A static support hierarchy represents which objects are likely to support which other objects on their surface (e.g., the floor supports tables, tables support plates).

Relation	$P(relation)$
inside(A,B)	$\frac{Vol(A \cap B)}{Vol(A)}$
right(A,B)	$\frac{Vol(A \cap \text{right}(B))}{Vol(A)}$
near(A,B)	$\mathbb{1}(dist(A, B) < t_{near})$

Table 1: Definitions of spatial relation using object bounding box computations.

thesis and containing about 12490 mostly indoor objects (Fisher et al., 2012). These models have text associated with them in the form of names and tags, and category labels. In addition, we assume the models have been scaled to physically plausible sizes and oriented with consistent up and front direction (Savva et al., 2014). All models are indexed in a database so they can be queried at run-time for retrieval.

3 System Description

We present how the parsed representations are used by our system to demonstrate the key issues that have to be addressed during text to scene generation. Our current implementation uses a simple deterministic approach to map text to the scene template and user actions on the scene. We use the Stanford CoreNLP pipeline[2] to process the input text and use rules to match dependency patterns.

3.1 Scene generation

During scene generation, we want to construct the most likely scene given the input text. We first parse the text into a scene template and use it to select appropriate models from the database. We then perform object layout and arrangement given the priors on spatial knowledge.

Scene Template Parsing We use the Stanford coreference system to determine when the same object is being referred to. To identify objects, we look for noun phrases and use the head word as the category, filtering with WordNet (Miller, 1995) to determine which objects are visualizable (under the physical object synset, excluding locations). To identify properties of the objects, we extract other adjectives and nouns in the noun phrase. We also match syntactic dependency patterns such as "X is made of Y" to extract more attributes and keywords. Finally, we use dependency patterns to extract spatial relations between objects.

[2] http://nlp.stanford.edu/software/corenlp.shtml

Figure 3: Select "a blue office chair" and "a wooden desk" from the models database

Object Selection Once we have the scene template, we use the keywords associated with each object to query the model database. We select randomly from the top 10 results for variety and to allow the user to regenerate the scene with different models. This step can be enhanced to take into account correlations between objects (e.g., a lamp on a table should not be a floor lamp model). See Figure 3 for an example of object selection.

Object Layout Given the selected models, the source scene template, and priors on spatial relations, we find an arrangement of the objects within the scene that maximizes the probability of the layout under the given scene template.

3.2 Scene Interaction

Here we address parsing of text after a scene has been generated and during interaction sessions.

Command Parsing We deterministically map verbs to possible actions as shown in Table 2. Multiple actions are possible for some verbs (e.g., "place" and "put" can refer to either $Move$ or $Insert$). To differentiate between these, we assume new objects are introduced with the indefinite article "a" whereas old ones are modified with the definite article "the".

Object Resolution To allow interaction with the scene, we must resolve references to objects within a scene. Objects are disambiguated by category and view-centric spatial relations. In addition to matching objects by their categories, we use the WordNet hierarchy to handle hyponym or hypernym referents. Depending on the current view, spatial relations such as "left" or "right" can refer to different objects (see Figure 4).

Scene Modification Based on the action we need to appropriately modify the current scene.

verb	Action	Example Text	Example Parse
generate	Generate	generate a room with a desk and a lamp	$Generate$({room,desk,lamp} , {}))
select	Select	select the chair on the right of the table	$Select$({lamp},{right(lamp,table)})
add, insert	Insert	add a lamp to the table	$Insert$({lamp},{on(lamp,table)})
delete, remove	Remove	remove the lamp	$Remove$({lamp})
move	Move	move the chair to the left	$Move$({chair},{left(chair)})
place, put	Move, Insert	put the lamp on the table	$Move$({lamp},{on(lamp,table)})
replace	Replace	replace the lamp with a vase	$Replace$({lamp},{vase})

Table 2: Mapping of verbs to possible actions.

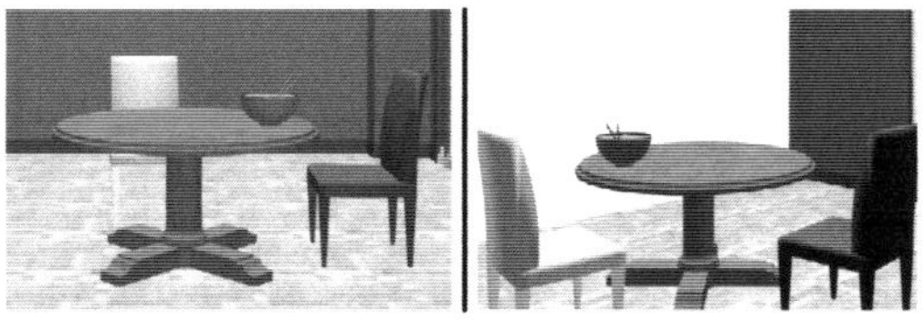

Figure 4: **Left**: chair is selected by "chair to the right of the table" or "object to the right of the table", but not selected by "cup to the right of the table". **Right**: Different view results in a different chair selection for "chair to the right of the table".

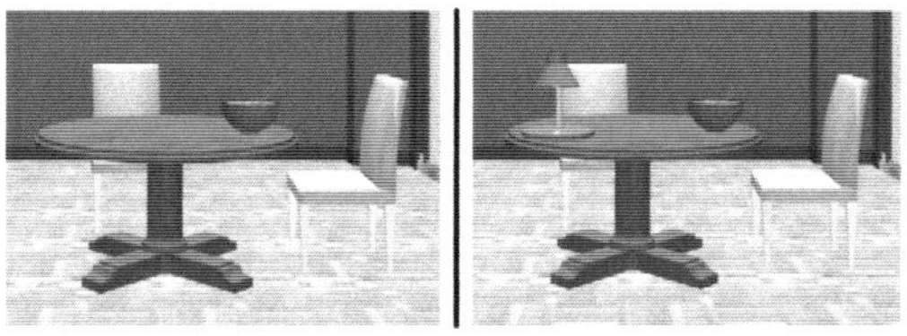

Figure 5: **Left**: initial scene. **Right**: after input "Put a lamp on the table".

We do this by maximizing the probability of a new scene template given the requested action and previous scene template (see Figure 5 for an example).

4 Future Directions

We described a system prototype to motivate approaching text to scene generation as a semantic parsing application. While this prototype illustrates inference of implicit constraints using prior knowledge, it still relies on hand coded rules for mapping text to the scene representation. This is similar to most previous work on text to scene generation (Winograd, 1972; Coyne and Sproat, 2001) and limits handling of natural language. More recently, (Zitnick et al., 2013) used data to learn how to ground sentences to a CRF representing 2D clipart scenes. Similarly, we plan to investigate using data to learn how to ground sentences to 3D scenes.

Spatial knowledge can be helpful for resolving ambiguities during parsing. For instance, from spatial priors of object positions and reasoning with physical constraints we can disambiguate the attachment of "next to" in "there is a book on the table next to the lamp". The book and lamp are likely on the table and thus $next\_to(book, lamp)$ should be more likely.

User interaction is a natural part of text to scene generation. We can leverage such interaction to obtain data for training a semantic parser. Every time the user issues a command, the user can indicate whether the result of the interaction was correct or not, and optionally provide a rating. By keeping track of these scene interactions and the user ratings we can construct a corpus of tuples containing: user action, parsed scene interaction, scene operation, scene state before and after the operation, and rating by the user. By building up such a corpus over multiple interactions and users, we obtain data for training semantic parsers.

References

Yoav Artzi and Luke Zettlemoyer. 2013. Weakly supervised learning of semantic parsers for mapping instructions to actions. *Transactions of the Association for Computational Linguistics*.

Bob Coyne and Richard Sproat. 2001. WordsEye: an automatic text-to-scene conversion system. In *Proceedings of the 28th annual conference on Computer graphics and interactive techniques*.

Matthew Fisher, Daniel Ritchie, Manolis Savva, Thomas Funkhouser, and Pat Hanrahan. 2012. Example-based synthesis of 3D object arrangements. *ACM Transactions on Graphics*.

Nicholas FitzGerald, Yoav Artzi, and Luke Zettlemoyer. 2013. Learning distributions over logical forms for referring expression generation. In *Proceedings of the Conference on EMNLP*.

Dave Golland, Percy Liang, and Dan Klein. 2010. A game-theoretic approach to generating spatial descriptions. In *Proceedings of the 2010 conference on EMNLP*.

Jayant Krishnamurthy and Thomas Kollar. 2013. Jointly learning to parse and perceive: Connecting natural language to the physical world. *Transactions of the Association for Computational Linguistics*.

Cynthia Matuszek, Nicholas Fitzgerald, Luke Zettlemoyer, Liefeng Bo, and Dieter Fox. 2012. A joint model of language and perception for grounded attribute learning. In *International Conference on Machine Learning*.

Cynthia Matuszek, Evan Herbst, Luke Zettlemoyer, and Dieter Fox. 2013. Learning to parse natural language commands to a robot control system. In *Experimental Robotics*.

G.A. Miller. 1995. WordNet: a lexical database for english. *CACM*.

Manolis Savva, Angel X. Chang, Gilbert Bernstein, Christopher D. Manning, and Pat Hanrahan. 2014. On being the right scale: Sizing large collections of 3D models. *Stanford University Technical Report CSTR 2014-03*.

Stefanie Tellex, Pratiksha Thaker, Joshua Joseph, and Nicholas Roy. 2014. Learning perceptually grounded word meanings from unaligned parallel data. *Machine Learning*.

Terry Winograd. 1972. Understanding natural language. *Cognitive psychology*.

C. Lawrence Zitnick, Devi Parikh, and Lucy Vanderwende. 2013. Learning the visual interpretation of sentences. In *IEEE Intenational Conference on Computer Vision (ICCV)*.

A Deep Architecture for Semantic Parsing

Edward Grefenstette, Phil Blunsom, Nando de Freitas and **Karl Moritz Hermann**
Department of Computer Science
University of Oxford, UK
{edwgre, pblunsom, nando, karher}@cs.ox.ac.uk

Abstract

Many successful approaches to semantic parsing build on top of the syntactic analysis of text, and make use of distributional representations or statistical models to match parses to ontology-specific queries. This paper presents a novel deep learning architecture which provides a semantic parsing system through the union of two neural models of language semantics. It allows for the generation of ontology-specific queries from natural language statements and questions without the need for parsing, which makes it especially suitable to grammatically malformed or syntactically atypical text, such as tweets, as well as permitting the development of semantic parsers for resource-poor languages.

1 Introduction

The ubiquity of always-online computers in the form of smartphones, tablets, and notebooks has boosted the demand for effective question answering systems. This is exemplified by the growing popularity of products like Apple's Siri or Google's Google Now services. In turn, this creates the need for increasingly sophisticated methods for semantic parsing. Recent work (Artzi and Zettlemoyer, 2013; Kwiatkowski et al., 2013; Matuszek et al., 2012; Liang et al., 2011, *inter alia*) has answered this call by progressively moving away from strictly rule-based semantic parsing, towards the use of distributed representations in conjunction with traditional grammatically-motivated re-write rules. This paper seeks to extend this line of thinking to its logical conclusion, by providing the first (to our knowledge) entirely distributed neural semantic generative parsing model. It does so by adapting deep learning methods from related work in sentiment analysis (Socher et al., 2012; Hermann and Blunsom, 2013), document classification (Yih et al., 2011; Lauly et al., 2014; Hermann and Blunsom, 2014a), frame-semantic parsing (Hermann et al., 2014), and machine translation (Mikolov et al., 2010; Kalchbrenner and Blunsom, 2013a), *inter alia*, combining two empirically successful deep learning models to form a new architecture for semantic parsing.

The structure of this short paper is as follows. We first provide a brief overview of the background literature this model builds on in §2. In §3, we begin by introducing two deep learning models with different aims, namely the joint learning of embeddings in parallel corpora, and the generation of strings of a language conditioned on a latent variable, respectively. We then discuss how both models can be combined and jointly trained to form a deep learning model supporting the generation of knowledgebase queries from natural language questions. Finally, in §4 we conclude by discussing planned experiments and the data requirements to effectively train this model.

2 Background

Semantic parsing describes a task within the larger field of natural language understanding. Within computational linguistics, semantic parsing is typically understood to be the task of mapping natural language sentences to formal representations of their underlying meaning. This semantic representation varies significantly depending on the task context. For instance, semantic parsing has been applied to interpreting movement instructions (Artzi and Zettlemoyer, 2013) or robot control (Matuszek et al., 2012), where the underlying representation would consist of actions.

Within the context of question answering—the focus of this paper—semantic parsing typically aims to map natural language to database queries that would answer a given question. Kwiatkowski

Proceedings of the ACL 2014 Workshop on Semantic Parsing, pages 22–27,
Baltimore, Maryland USA, June 26 2014.

et al. (2013) approach this problem using a multi-step model. First, they use a CCG-like parser to convert natural language into an underspecified logical form (ULF). Second, the ULF is converted into a specified form (here a FreeBase query), which can be used to lookup the answer to the given natural language question.

3 Model Description

We describe a semantic-parsing model that learns to derive quasi-logical database queries from natural language. The model follows the structure of Kwiatkowski et al. (2013), but relies on a series of neural networks and distributed representations in lieu of the CCG and λ-Calculus based representations used in that paper.

The model described here borrows heavily from two approaches in the deep learning literature. First, a noise-contrastive neural network similar to that of Hermann and Blunsom (2014a, 2014b) is used to learn a joint latent representation for natural language and database queries (§3.1). Second, we employ a structured conditional neural language model in §3.2 to generate queries given such latent representations. Below we provide the necessary background on these two components, before introducing the combined model and describing its learning setup.

3.1 Bilingual Compositional Sentence Models

The bilingual compositional sentence model (BiCVM) of Hermann and Blunsom (2014a) provides a state-of-the-art method for learning semantically informative distributed representations for sentences of language pairs from parallel corpora. Through the joint production of a shared latent representation for semantically aligned sentence pairs, it optimises sentence embeddings so that the respective representations of dissimilar cross-lingual sentence pairs will be weakly aligned, while those of similar sentence pairs will be strongly aligned. Both the ability to jointly learn sentence embeddings, and to produce latent shared representations, will be relevant to our semantic parsing pipeline.

The BiCVM model shown in Fig. 1 assumes vector composition functions g and h, which map an ordered set of vectors (here, word embeddings from $\mathcal{D}_A, \mathcal{D}_B$) onto a single vector in $\mathbb{R}^n$. As stated above, for semantically equivalent sentences a, b across languages $\mathcal{L}_A, \mathcal{L}_B$, the model aims to minimise the distance between these composed representations:

$$E_{bi}(a, b) = \|g(a) - h(b)\|^2$$

In order to avoid strong alignment between dissimilar cross-lingual sentence pairs, this error is combined with a noise-contrastive hinge loss, where $n \in \mathcal{L}_B$ is a randomly sampled sentence, dissimilar to the parallel pair $\{a, b\}$, and m denotes some margin:

$$E_{hl}(a, b, n) = [m + E_{bi}(a, b) - E_{bi}(a, n)]_+ ,$$

where $[x]_+ = max(0, x)$. The resulting objective function is as follows

$$J(\theta) = \sum_{(a,b)\in C} \left(\sum_{i=1}^{k} E_{hl}(a, b, n_i) + \frac{\lambda}{2}\|\theta\|^2 \right),$$

with $\frac{\lambda}{2}\|\theta\|^2$ as the L_2 regularization term and $\theta = \{g, h, \mathcal{D}_A, \mathcal{D}_B\}$ as the set of model variables.

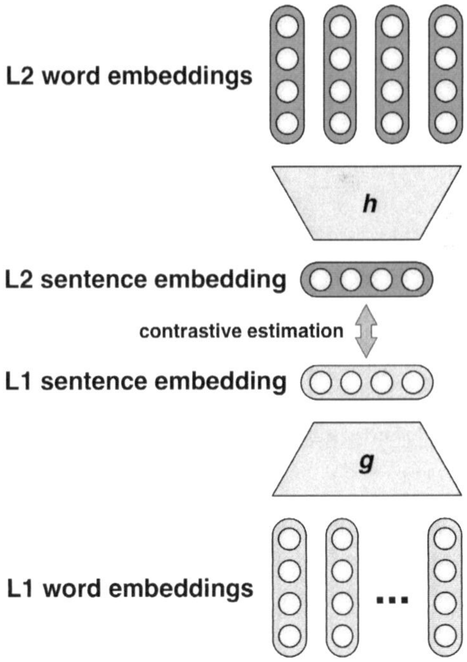

Figure 1: Diagrammatic representation of a BiCVM.

While Hermann and Blunsom (2014a) applied this model only to parallel corpora of sentences, it is important to note that the model is agnostic concerning the inputs of functions g and h. In this paper we will discuss how this model can be applied to non-sentential inputs.

3.2 Conditional Neural Language Models

Neural language models (Bengio et al., 2006) provide a distributed alternative to n-gram language models, permitting the joint learning of a prediction function for the next word in a sequence given the distributed representations of a subset of the last $n-1$ words alongside the representations themselves. Recent work in dialogue act labelling (Kalchbrenner and Blunsom, 2013b) and in machine translation (Kalchbrenner and Blunsom, 2013a) has demonstrated that a particular kind of neural language model based on recurrent neural networks (Mikolov et al., 2010; Sutskever et al., 2011) could be extended so that the next word in a sequence is jointly generated by the word history and the distributed representation for a conditioning element, such as the dialogue class of a previous sentence, or the vector representation of a source sentence. In this section, we briefly describe a general formulation of conditional neural language models, based on the log-bilinear models of Mnih and Hinton (2007) due to their relative simplicity.

A log-bilinear language model is a neural network modelling a probability distribution over the next word in a sequence given the previous $n-1$, i.e. $p(w_n|w_{1:n-1})$. Let $|V|$ be the size of our vocabulary, and R be a $|V| \times d$ vocabulary matrix where the R_{w_i} demnotes the row containing the word embedding in $\mathbb{R}^d$ of a word w_i, with d being a hyper-parameter indicating embedding size. Let C_i be the context transform matrix in $\mathbb{R}^{d\times d}$ which modifies the representation of the ith word in the word history. Let b_{w_i} be a scalar bias associated with a word w_i, and b_R be a bias vector in $\mathbb{R}^d$ associated with the model. A log-bilinear model expressed the probability of w_n given a history of $n-1$ words as a function of the energy of the network:

$$E(w_n; w_{1:n-1}) = - \left(\sum_{i=1}^{n-1} R_{w_i}^T C_i \right) R_{w_n} - b_R^T R_{w_n} - b_{w_n}$$

From this, the probability distribution over the next word is obtained:

$$p(w_n|w_{1:n-1}) = \frac{e^{-E(w_n;w_{1:n-1})}}{\sum_{w_n} e^{-E(w_n;w_{1:n-1})}}$$

To reframe a log-bilinear language model as a conditional language model (CNLM), illustrated

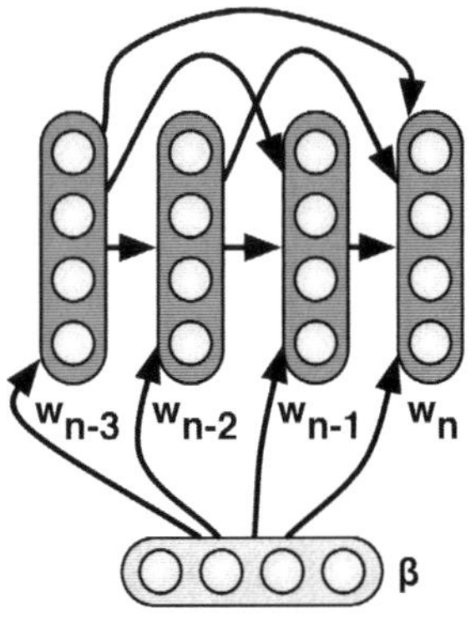

Figure 2: Diagrammatic representation of a Conditional Neural Language Model.

in Fig. 2, let us suppose that we wish to jointly condition the next word on its history and some variable β, for which an embedding r_β has been obtained through a previous step, in order to compute $p(w_n|w_{1:n-1}, \beta)$. The simplest way to do this additively, which allows us to treat the contribution of the embedding for β as similar to that of an extra word in the history. We define a new energy function:

$$E(w_n; w_{1:n-1}, \beta) = - \left(\left(\sum_{i=1}^{n-1} R_{w_i}^T C_i \right) + r_\beta^T C_\beta \right) R_{w_n} - b_R^T R_{w_n} - b_{w_n}$$

to obtain the probability

$$p(w_n|w_{1:n-1}, \beta) = \frac{e^{-E(w_n;w_{1:n-1},\beta)}}{\sum_{w_n} e^{-E(w_n;w_{1:n-1},\beta)}}$$

Log-bilinear language models and their conditional variants alike are typically trained by maximising the log-probability of observed sequences.

3.3 A Combined Semantic Parsing Model

The models in §§3.1–3.2 can be combined to form a model capable of jointly learning a shared latent representation for question/query pairs using a BiCVM, and using this latent representation to learn a conditional log-bilinear CNLM. The full model is shown in Fig. 3. Here, we explain the final model architecture both for training and for subsequent use as a generative model. The details of the training procedure will be discussed in §3.4.

The combination is fairly straightforward, and happens in two steps at training time. For the

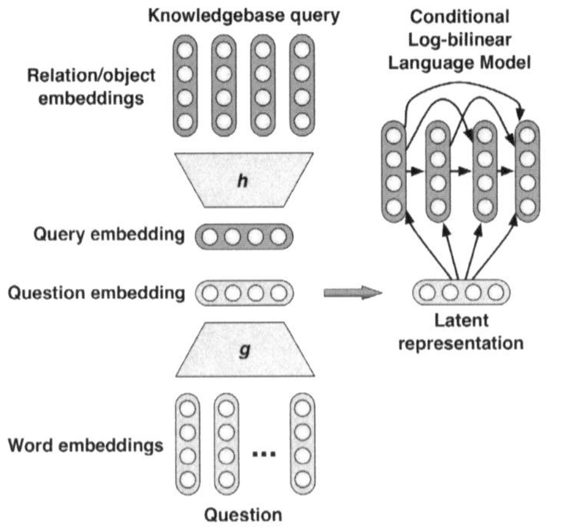

Figure 3: Diagrammatic representation of the full model. First the mappings for obtaining latent forms of questions and queries are jointly learned through a BiCVM. The latent form for questions then serves as conditioning element in a log-bilinear CNLM.

first step, shown in the left hand side of Fig. 3, a BiCVM is trained against a parallel corpora of natural language question and knowledgebase query pairs. Optionally, the embeddings for the query symbol representations and question words are initialised and/or fine-tuned during training, as discussed in §3.4. For the natural language side of the model, the composition function g can be a simple additive model as in Hermann and Blunsom (2014a), although the semantic information required for the task proposed here would probably benefit from a more complex composition function such as a convolution neural network. Function h, which maps the knowledgebase queries into the shared space could also rely on convolution, although the structure of the database queries might favour a setup relying primarily on bi-gram composition.

Using function g and the original training data, the training data for the second stage is created by obtaining the latent representation for the questions of the original dataset. We thereby obtain pairs of aligned latent question representations and knowledgebase queries. This data allows us to train a log-bilinear CNLM as shown on the right side of Fig. 3.

Once trained, the models can be fully joined to produce a generative neural network as shown in Fig. 4. The network modelling g from the BiCVM takes the distributed representations of question words from unseen questions, and produces a latent representation. The latent representation is then passed to the log-bilinear CNLM, which conditionally generates a knowledgebase query corresponding to the question.

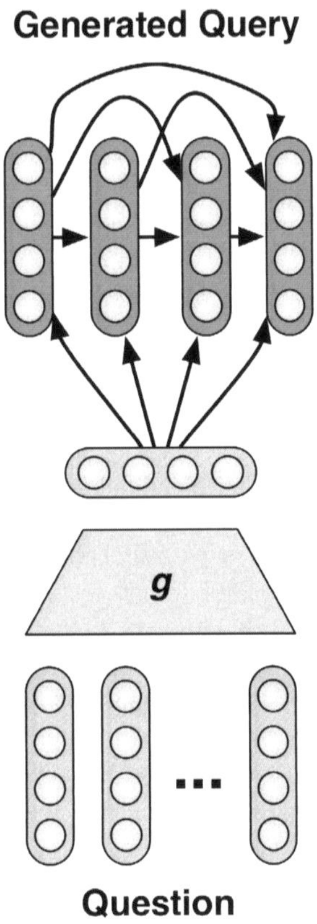

Figure 4: Diagrammatic representation of the final network. The question-compositional segment of the BiCVM produces a latent representation, conditioning a CNLM generating a query.

3.4 Learning Model Parameters

We propose training the model of §3.3 in a two stage process, in line with the symbolic model of Kwiatkowski et al. (2013).

First, a BiCVM is trained on a parallel corpus C of question-query pairs $\langle Q, R \rangle \in C$, using composition functions g for natural language questions and h for database queries. While functions g and h may differ from those discussed in Hermann and Blunsom (2014a), the basic noise-contrastive optimisation function remains the same. It is possible to initialise the model fully randomly, in which case the model parameters θ learned at this stage include the two distributed representation lexica for questions and queries, $\mathcal{D}_Q$ and $\mathcal{D}_R$ respectively, as well as all parameters for g and h.

Alternatively, word embeddings in $\mathcal{D}_Q$ could be initialised with representations learned separately, for instance with a neural language model or a similar system (Mikolov et al., 2010; Turian et al., 2010; Collobert et al., 2011, *inter alia*). Likewise, the relation and object embeddings in $\mathcal{D}_R$ could be initialised with representations learned from distributed relation extraction schemas such as that of Riedel et al. (2013).

Having learned representations for queries in $\mathcal{D}_R$ as well as function g, the second training phase of the model uses a new parallel corpus consisting of pairs $\langle g(Q), R\rangle \in C'$ to train the CNLM as presented in §3.3.

The two training steps can be applied iteratively, and further, it is trivial to modify the learning procedure to use composition function h as another input for the CNLM training phrase in an autoencoder-like setup.

4 Experimental Requirements and Further Work

The particular training procedure for the model described in this paper requires aligned question/knowledgebase query pairs. There exist some small corpora that could be used for this task (Zelle and Mooney, 1996; Cai and Yates, 2013). In order to scale training beyond these small corpora, we hypothesise that larger amounts of (potentially noisy) training data could be obtained using a boot-strapping technique similar to Kwiatkowski et al. (2013).

To evaluate this model, we will follow the experimental setup of Kwiatkowski et al. (2013). With the provisio that the model can generate freebase queries correctly, further work will seek to determine whether this architecture can generate other structured formal language expressions, such as lambda expressions for use in textual entailement tasks.

Acknowledgements

This work was supported by a Xerox Foundation Award, EPSRC grants number EP/I03808X/1 and EP/K036580/1, and the Canadian Institute for Advanced Research (CIFAR) Program on Adaptive Perception and Neural Computation.

References

Yoav Artzi and Luke Zettlemoyer. 2013. Weakly supervised learning of semantic parsers for mapping instructions to actions. *Transactions of the Association for Computational Linguistics*, 1(1):49–62.

Yoshua Bengio, Holger Schwenk, Jean-Sébastien Senécal, Fréderic Morin, and Jean-Luc Gauvain. 2006. Neural probabilistic language models. In *Innovations in Machine Learning*, pages 137–186. Springer.

Qingqing Cai and Alexander Yates. 2013. Large-scale Semantic Parsing via Schema Matching and Lexicon Extension. In *Proceedings of the Annual Meeting of the Association for Computational Linguistics (ACL)*.

Ronan Collobert, Jason Weston, Leon Bottou, Michael Karlen, Koray Kavukcuoglu, and Pavel Kuksa. 2011. Natural language processing (almost) from scratch. *Journal of Machine Learning Research*, 12:2493–2537.

Karl Moritz Hermann and Phil Blunsom. 2013. The Role of Syntax in Vector Space Models of Compositional Semantics. In *Proceedings of the 51st Annual Meeting of the Association for Computational Linguistics (Volume 1: Long Papers)*, Sofia, Bulgaria, August. Association for Computational Linguistics.

Karl Moritz Hermann and Phil Blunsom. 2014a. Multilingual Distributed Representations without Word Alignment. In *Proceedings of the 2nd International Conference on Learning Representations*, Banff, Canada, April.

Karl Moritz Hermann and Phil Blunsom. 2014b. Multilingual Models for Compositional Distributional Semantics. In *Proceedings of the 52nd Annual Meeting of the Association for Computational Linguistics (Volume 1: Long Papers)*, Baltimore, USA, June. Association for Computational Linguistics.

Karl Moritz Hermann, Dipanjan Das, Jason Weston, and Kuzman Ganchev. 2014. Semantic Frame Identification with Distributed Word Representations. In *Proceedings of the 52nd Annual Meeting of the Association for Computational Linguistics (Volume 1: Long Papers)*, Baltimore, USA, June. Association for Computational Linguistics.

Nal Kalchbrenner and Phil Blunsom. 2013a. Recurrent continuous translation models. In *Proceedings of the 2013 Conference on Empirical Methods in Natural Language Processing (EMNLP), Seattle, USA. Association for Computational Linguistics*.

Nal Kalchbrenner and Phil Blunsom. 2013b. Recurrent convolutional neural networks for discourse compositionality. *arXiv preprint arXiv:1306.3584*.

Tom Kwiatkowski, Eunsol Choi, Yoav Artzi, and Luke Zettlemoyer. 2013. Scaling semantic parsers with on-the-fly ontology matching. In *Proceedings of the 2013 Conference on Empirical Methods in Natural Language Processing*, pages 1545–1556, Seattle, Washington, USA, October. Association for Computational Linguistics.

Stanislas Lauly, Alex Boulanger, and Hugo Larochelle. 2014. Learning multilingual word representations using a bag-of-words autoencoder. *CoRR*, abs/1401.1803.

Percy Liang, Michael I. Jordan, and Dan Klein. 2011. Learning dependency-based compositional semantics. In *Proceedings of the 49th Annual Meeting of the Association for Computational Linguistics: Human Language Technologies - Volume 1*, HLT '11, pages 590–599, Stroudsburg, PA, USA. Association for Computational Linguistics.

Cynthia Matuszek, Nicholas FitzGerald, Luke S. Zettlemoyer, Liefeng Bo, and Dieter Fox. 2012. A joint model of language and perception for grounded attribute learning. In *Proceedings of the 29th International Conference on Machine Learning, ICML 2012, Edinburgh, Scotland, UK, June 26 - July 1, 2012*.

Tomas Mikolov, Martin Karafiát, Lukas Burget, Jan Cernockỳ, and Sanjeev Khudanpur. 2010. Recurrent neural network based language model. In *INTERSPEECH*, pages 1045–1048.

Andriy Mnih and Geoffrey Hinton. 2007. Three new graphical models for statistical language modelling. In *Proceedings of the 24th international conference on Machine learning*, pages 641–648. ACM.

Sebastian Riedel, Limin Yao, Benjamin M. Marlin, and Andrew McCallum. 2013. Relation extraction with matrix factorization and universal schemas. In *Joint Human Language Technology Conference/Annual Meeting of the North American Chapter of the Association for Computational Linguistics (HLT-NAACL '13)*, June.

Richard Socher, Brody Huval, Christopher D. Manning, and Andrew Y. Ng. 2012. Semantic compositionality through recursive matrix-vector spaces. In *Proceedings of EMNLP-CoNLL*, pages 1201–1211.

Ilya Sutskever, James Martens, and Geoffrey E Hinton. 2011. Generating text with recurrent neural networks. In *Proceedings of the 28th International Conference on Machine Learning (ICML-11)*, pages 1017–1024.

Joseph Turian, Lev Ratinov, and Yoshua Bengio. 2010. Word representations: A simple and general method for semi-supervised learning. In *Proceedings of ACL*, Stroudsburg, PA, USA.

Wen-Tau Yih, Kristina Toutanova, John C. Platt, and Christopher Meek. 2011. Learning Discriminative Projections for Text Similarity Measures. In *Proceedings of the Fifteenth Conference on Computational Natural Language Learning*, CoNLL '11, pages 247–256, Stroudsburg, PA, USA. Association for Computational Linguistics.

John M. Zelle and Raymond J. Mooney. 1996. Learning to parse database queries using inductive logic programming. In *Proceedings of the National Conference on Artificial Intelligence*, pages 1050–1055.

Combining Formal and Distributional Models of Temporal and Intensional Semantics

Mike Lewis
School of Informatics
University of Edinburgh
Edinburgh, EH8 9AB, UK
mike.lewis@ed.ac.uk

Mark Steedman
School of Informatics
University of Edinburgh
Edinburgh, EH8 9AB, UK
steedman@inf.ed.ac.uk

Abstract

We outline a vision for computational semantics in which formal compositional semantics is combined with a powerful, structured lexical semantics derived from distributional statistics. We consider how existing work (Lewis and Steedman, 2013) could be extended with a much richer lexical semantics using recent techniques for modelling processes (Scaria et al., 2013)—for example, learning that *visiting* events start with *arriving* and end with *leaving*. We show how to closely integrate this information with theories of formal semantics, allowing complex compositional inferences such as *is visiting→has arrived in but will leave*, which requires interpreting both the function and content words. This will allow machine reading systems to understand not just *what* has happened, but *when*.

1 Combined Distributional and Logical Semantics

Distributional semantics aims to induce the meaning of language from unlabelled text. Traditional approaches to distributional semantics have represented semantics in vector spaces (Baroni et al., 2013). Words are assigned vectors based on collocations in large corpora, and then these vectors a composed into vectors representing longer utterances. However, so far there is relatively limited empirical evidence that composed vectors provide useful representations for whole sentences, and it is unclear how to represent logical operators (such as universal quantifiers) in a vector space. While future breakthroughs may overcome these limitations, there are already well developed solutions in the formal semantics literature using logical representations. On the other hand, standard formal semantic approaches such as Bos (2008) have found that hand-built ontologies such as WordNet (Miller, 1995) provide an insufficient model of lexical semantics, leading to low recall on applications. The complementary strengths and weaknesses of formal and distributional semantics motivate combining them into a single model.

In Lewis and Steedman (2013), we proposed a solution to these problems which uses CCG (Steedman, 2012) as a model of formal semantics, making it straightforward to build wide-coverage logical forms. Hand built representations are added for a small number of function words such as negatives and quantifiers—but the lexical semantics is represented by first clustering predicates (based on their usage in large corpora), and then using the cluster-identifiers as symbols in the logical form. For example, the induced CCG lexicon might contain entries such as the following[1]:

write $\vdash (S\backslash NP)/NP$
$: \lambda y \lambda x \lambda e.rel43(x, y, e)$

author $\vdash N/PP_{of}$
$: \lambda y \lambda x \lambda e.rel43(x, y, e)$

Equivalent sentences like *Shakespeare wrote Macbeth* and *Shakespeare is the author of Macbeth* can then both be mapped to a $rel43(shakespeare, macbeth)$ logical form, using derivations such as:

$$\begin{array}{ccc}
\text{Shakespeare} & \text{wrote} & \text{Macbeth} \\
\hline
NP & (S\backslash NP)/NP & NP \\
shakespeare & \lambda y\lambda x\lambda e.rel43(x,y,e) & macbeth \\
 & \multicolumn{2}{c}{\overline{\qquad\qquad\qquad\qquad}^{>}} \\
 & \multicolumn{2}{c}{S\backslash NP} \\
 & \multicolumn{2}{c}{\lambda x\lambda e.rel43(x, macbeth, e)} \\
\multicolumn{3}{c}{\overline{\qquad\qquad\qquad\qquad\qquad\qquad}^{<}} \\
\multicolumn{3}{c}{S} \\
\multicolumn{3}{c}{\lambda e.rel43(shakespeare, macbeth, e)}
\end{array}$$

This approach interacts seamlessly with standard formal semantics—for example modelling negation by mapping *Francis Bacon didn't write Macbeth* to $\neg rel43(francis\_bacon, macbeth)$. Their method has shown good performance on a dataset of multi-sentence textual inference problems involving quantifiers, by using first-order the-

[1] The e variables are Davidsonian event variables.

Proceedings of the ACL 2014 Workshop on Semantic Parsing, pages 28–32,
Baltimore, Maryland USA, June 26 2014.

orem proving. Ambiguity is handled by a probabilistic model, based on the types of the nouns.

Beltagy et al. (2013) use an alternative approach with similar goals, in which every word instance expresses a unique semantic primitive, but is connected to the meanings of other word instances using distributionally-derived probabilistic inference rules. This approach risks requiring very large number of inference rules, which may make inference inefficient. Our approach avoid this problem by attempting to fully represent lexical semantics in the lexicon.

2 Proposal

We propose how our previous model could be extended to make more sophisticated inferences. We will demonstrate how many interesting problems in semantics could be solved with a system based on three components:

- A CCG syntactic parse for modelling composition. Using CCG allows us to handle interesting forms of composition, such as coordination, extraction, questions, right node raising, etc. CCG also has both a developed theory of operator semantics and a transparent interface to the underlying predicate argument structure.
- A small hand built lexicon for words with complex semantics—such as negatives, quantifiers, modals, and implicative verbs.
- A rich model of lexical semantics derived from distributionally-induced entailment graphs (Berant et al., 2011), extended with subcategories of entailment relations in a similar way to Scaria et al. (2013). We show how such graphs can be converted into a CCG lexicon.

2.1 Directional Inference

A major limitation of our previous model is that it uses a flat clustering to model the meaning of content words. This method enables them to model synonymy relations between words, but not relations where the entailment only holds in one direction—for example, *conquers→invades*, but not vice-versa. This problem can be addressed using the *entailment graph* framework introduced by Berant et al. (2011), which learns globally consistent graphs over predicates in which directed edges indicate entailment relations. Exactly the same methods can be used to build entailment graphs over the predicates derived from a CCG parse:

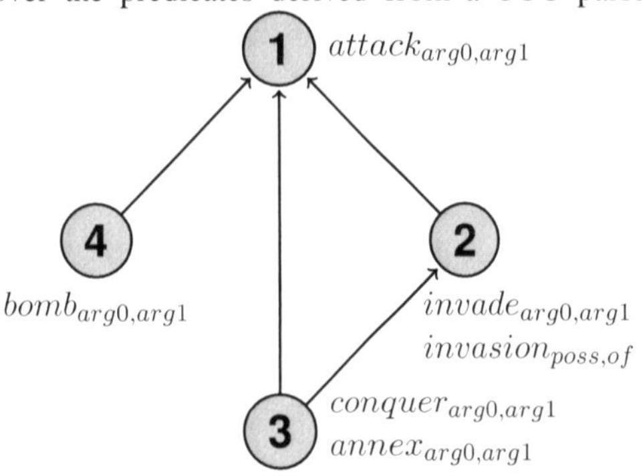

The graph can then be converted to a CCG lexicon by making the semantics of a word be the conjunction of all the relation identifiers it implies in the graph. For example, the above graph is equivalent to the following lexicon:

attack $\vdash (S\backslash NP)/NP$
$: \lambda x \lambda y \lambda e.rel1(x,y,e)$
bomb $\vdash (S\backslash NP)/NP$
$: \lambda x \lambda y \lambda e.rel1(x,y,e) \wedge rel4(x,y,e)$
invade $\vdash (S\backslash NP)/NP$
$: \lambda x \lambda y \lambda e.rel1(x,y,e) \wedge rel2(x,y,e)$
conquer $\vdash (S\backslash NP)/NP$
$: \lambda x \lambda y \lambda e.rel1(x,y,e) \wedge rel2(x,y,e) \wedge rel3(x,y,e)$

This lexicon supports the correct inferences, such as *conquers→attacks* and *didn't invade→didn't conquer*.

2.2 Temporal Semantics

One case where combining formal and distributional semantics may be particularly helpful is in giving a detailed model of temporal semantics. A rich understanding of time would allow us to understand *when* events took place, or when states were true. Most existing work ignores tense, and would treat the expressions *used to be president* and *is president* either as equivalent or completely unrelated. Failing to model tense would lead to incorrect inferences when answering questions such as *Who is the president of the USA?*

Another motivation for considering a detailed model of temporal semantics is that understanding the time of events should improve the quality of the distributional clustering. It has recently been shown that such information is extremely useful for learning equivalences between predicates, by determining which sentences describe the same events using date-stamped text and simple tense heuristics (Zhang and Weld, 2013). Such methods escape common problems with traditional approaches to distributional similarity, such as conflating causes with effects, and may prove very useful for building entailment graphs.

Temporal information is conveyed by both by auxiliary verbs such as *will* or *used to*, and in the semantics of content words. For example, the statement *John is visiting Baltimore* licences entailments such as *John has arrived in Baltimore* and *John will leave Baltimore*, which can only be understood through both knowledge of tense and lexical semantic relations.

The requisite information about lexical semantics could be represented by labelling edges in the entailment graphs, along the lines of Scaria et al. (2013). Instead of edges simply representing entailment, they should represent different kinds of lexical relations, such as *precondition* or *consequence*. Building such graphs requires training classifiers that predict fine-grained semantic relations between predicates, and defining transitivity properties of the relations (e.g. a precondition of a precondition is a precondition). For example, the system might learn the following graph:

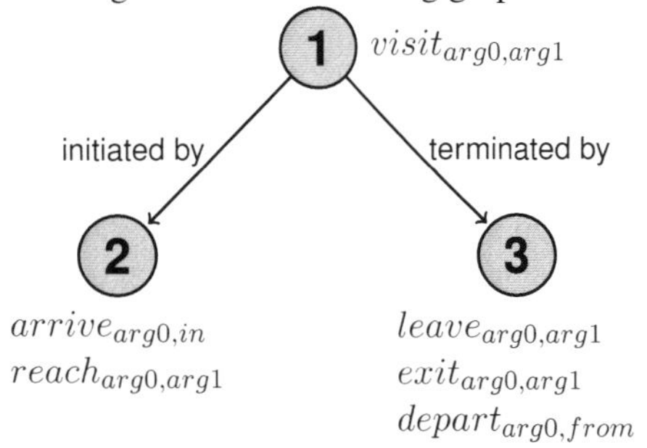

By defining a simple mapping between edge labels and logical forms, this graph can be converted to CCG lexical entries such as:

visit $\vdash (S\backslash NP)/NP$
$: \lambda y \lambda x \lambda e.rel1(x,y,e) \wedge \exists e'[rel2(x,y,e') \wedge before(e,e')] \wedge \exists e''[rel3(x,y,e'') \wedge after(e,e'')]$

arrive $\vdash (S\backslash NP)/PP_{in}$
$: \lambda y \lambda x \lambda e.rel2(x,y,e)$

leave $\vdash (S\backslash NP)/NP$
$: \lambda y \lambda x \lambda e.rel3(x,y,e)$

These lexical entries could be complemented with hand-built interpretations for a small set of common auxiliary verbs:

has $\vdash (S\backslash NP)/(S_b\backslash NP)$
$: \lambda p \lambda x \lambda e.before(r,e) \wedge p(x,e)$

will $\vdash (S\backslash NP)/(S_b\backslash NP)$
$: \lambda p \lambda x \lambda e.after(r,e) \wedge p(x,e)$

is $\vdash (S\backslash NP)/(S_{ng}\backslash NP)$
$: \lambda p \lambda x \lambda e.during(r,e) \wedge p(x,e)$

used $\vdash (S\backslash NP)/(S_{to}\backslash NP)$
$: \lambda p \lambda x \lambda e.before(r,e) \wedge p(x,e) \wedge \neg\exists e'[during(r) \wedge p(x,e')]$

Here, r is the reference time (e.g. the time that the news article was written). It is easy to verify that such a lexicon supports inferences such as *is visiting→will leave*, *has visited→has arrived in*, or *used to be president→is not president.*

The model described here only discusses tense, not aspect—so does not distinguish between *John arrived in Baltimore* and *John has arrived in Baltimore* (the latter says that the consequences of his arrival still hold—i.e. that he is still in Baltimore). Going further, we could implement the much more detailed proposal of Moens and Steedman (1988). Building this model would require distinguishing *states* from *events*—for example, the semantics of *arrive*, *visit* and *leave* could all be expressed in terms of the times that an *is in* state holds.

2.3 Intensional Semantics

Similar work could be done by subcategorizing edges in the graph with other lexical relations. For example, we could extend the graph with *goal* relations between words, such as between *set out for* and *arrive in*, *search* and *find*, or *invade* and *conquer*:

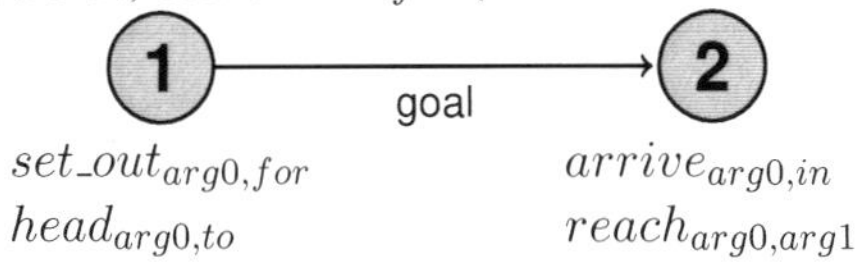

The corresponding lexicon contains entries such as:

set out $\vdash (S\backslash NP)/PP_{for}$
$: \lambda y \lambda x \lambda e.rel1(x,y,e) \wedge \diamond\exists e'[goal(e,e') \wedge rel2(x,y,e')]$

The modal logic $\diamond$ operator is used to mark that the goal event is a hypothetical proposition, that is not asserted to be true in the real world—so *Columbus set out for India↛Columbus reached India*. The same mechanism allows us to handle Montague (1973)'s example that *John seeks a unicorn* does not imply the existence of a unicorn.

Just as temporal information can be expressed by auxiliary verbs, relations such as goals can

Columbus	failed	to	reach India
$S_{dcl}/(S_{dcl}\backslash NP)$	$(S_{dcl}\backslash NP)/(S_{to}\backslash NP)$	$(S_{to}\backslash NP)/(S_b\backslash NP)$	$S_b\backslash NP$
$\lambda p.p(Columbus)$	$\lambda p\lambda x\lambda e.\diamond\exists e'[p(x,e')\wedge goal(e',e)]\wedge\neg\exists e''[p(x,e'')]$	$\lambda p\lambda x\lambda e.p(x,e)$	$\lambda x\lambda e.rel2(x,India,e)$

$$\frac{}{S_{to}\backslash NP \quad \lambda x\lambda e.rel2(x,India,e)}>$$

$$\frac{}{S_{dcl}\backslash NP \quad \lambda x\lambda e.\diamond\exists e'[rel2(x,India,e')\wedge goal(e',e)]\wedge\neg\exists e''[rel2(x,India,e'')]}>$$

$$\frac{}{S_{dcl} \quad \lambda e.\diamond\exists e'[rel2(Columbus,India,e')\wedge goal(e',e)]\wedge\neg\exists e''[rel2(Columbus,India,e'')]}>$$

Figure 1: Output from our system for the sentence *Columbus failed to reach India*

be expressed using implicative verbs like *try* or *fail*. As the semantics of implicative verbs is often complex (Karttunen, 1971), we propose hand-coding their lexical entries:

try $\vdash (S\backslash NP)/(S_{to}\backslash NP)$
$: \lambda p\lambda x\lambda e.\diamond\exists e'[goal(e,e')\wedge p(x,e')]$

fail $\vdash (S\backslash NP)/(S_{to}\backslash NP)$
$: \lambda p\lambda x\lambda e.\diamond\exists e'[goal(e,e')\wedge p(x,e')]\wedge$
$\neg\exists e''[goal(e,e'')\wedge p(x,e'')]$

The $\diamond$ operator is used to assert that the complement of *try* is a hypothetical proposition (so *try to reach$\not\rightarrow$reach*). Our semantics for *fail* is the same as that for *try*, except that it asserts that the goal event did not occur in the real world.

These lexical entries allow us to make complex compositional inferences, for example *Columbus failed to reach India* now entails *Columbus set out for India*, *Columbus tried to reach India* and *Columbus didn't arrive in India*.

Again, we expect that the improved model of formal semantics should increase the quality of the entailment graphs, by allowing us to only cluster predicates based on their real-world arguments (ignoring hypothetical events).

3 Conclusion

We have argued that several promising recent threads of research in semantics can be combined into a single model. The model we have described would enable wide-coverage mapping of open-domain text onto rich logical forms that model complex aspects of semantics such as negation, quantification, modality and tense—whilst also using a robust distributional model of lexical semantics that captures the structure of events. Considering these interwined issues would allow complex compositional inferences which are far beyond the current state of the art, and would give a more powerful model for natural language understanding.

Acknowledgements

We thank Omri Abend, Michael Roth and the anonymous reviewers for their helpful comments. This work was funded by ERC Advanced Fellowship 249520 GRAMPLUS and IP EC-FP7-270273 Xperience.

References

M. Baroni, R. Bernardi, and R. Zamparelli. 2013. Frege in space: A program for compositional distributional semantics. *Linguistic Issues in Language Technologies*.

Islam Beltagy, Cuong Chau, Gemma Boleda, Dan Garrette, Katrin Erk, and Raymond Mooney. 2013. Montague meets markov: Deep semantics with probabilistic logical form. pages 11–21, June.

Jonathan Berant, Ido Dagan, and Jacob Goldberger. 2011. Global learning of typed entailment rules. In *Proceedings of the 49th Annual Meeting of the Association for Computational Linguistics: Human Language Technologies - Volume 1*, HLT '11, pages 610–619. Association for Computational Linguistics.

Johan Bos. 2008. Wide-coverage semantic analysis with boxer. In Johan Bos and Rodolfo Delmonte, editors, *Semantics in Text Processing. STEP 2008 Conference Proceedings*, Research in Computational Semantics, pages 277–286. College Publications.

L. Karttunen. 1971. *The Logic of English Predicate Complement Constructions*. Linguistics Club Bloomington, Ind: IU Linguistics Club. Indiana University Linguistics Club.

Mike Lewis and Mark Steedman. 2013. Combined Distributional and Logical Semantics. *Transactions of the Association for Computational Linguistics*, 1:179–192.

G.A. Miller. 1995. Wordnet: a lexical database for english. *Communications of the ACM*, 38(11):39–41.

Marc Moens and Mark Steedman. 1988. Temporal ontology and temporal reference. *Computational linguistics*, 14(2):15–28.

Richard Montague. 1973. The proper treatment of quantification in ordinary english. In *Approaches to natural language*, pages 221–242. Springer.

Aju Thalappillil Scaria, Jonathan Berant, Mengqiu Wang, Peter Clark, Justin Lewis, Brittany Harding, and Christopher D. Manning. 2013. Learning biological processes with global constraints. In *Proceedings of EMNLP*.

Mark Steedman. 2012. *Taking Scope: The Natural Semantics of Quantifiers*. MIT Press.

Congle Zhang and Daniel S Weld. 2013. Harvesting parallel news streams to generate paraphrases of event relations.

Cooking with Semantics

Jon Malmaud
Brain and Cognitive Sciences
MIT
43 Vassar St.
Cambridge, MA
malmaud@mit.edu

Earl J. Wagner, Nancy Chang, Kevin Murphy
Google
1600 Amphitheatre Pkwy
Mountain View, CA
wag@google.com, ncchang@google.com, kpmurphy@google.com

Abstract

We are interested in the automatic interpretation of how-to instructions, such as cooking recipes, into semantic representations that can facilitate sophisticated question answering. Recent work has shown impressive results on semantic parsing of instructions with minimal supervision, but such techniques cannot handle much of the situated and ambiguous language used in instructions found on the web. In this paper, we suggest how to extend such methods using a model of pragmatics, based on a rich representation of world state.

1 Introduction

Understanding instructional text found on the web presents unique challenges and opportunities that represent a frontier for semantic parsing. Crucially, instructional language is *situated*: it assumes a situational context within which the agent (i.e., the reader) is to carry out a sequence of actions, as applied to objects that are (or become) available in the immediate environment. These actions and objects may not be explicitly specified; indeed, much instructional language is ambiguous, underspecified and often even ungrammatical relative to conventional usage.

In this "vision paper", we focus on interpreting cooking recipes. While there are several services that already support searching for recipes (such as Google Recipe Search[1], Yummly, Foodily, and MyTaste), the faceted search capabilities they provide are limited to recipe meta-data such as ingredients, genres, cooking time, portions, and nutrition values. Some of this information is explicitly marked up in machine-readable form[2]. However, the actual steps of the recipe are treated as an unstructured blob of text. (The same problem applies to other instructional sites, such as ehow.com, wikihow.com, answers.yahoo.com, www.instructables.com, etc.) Interpreting the steps of recipes (and instructions more generally) is the goal of this paper.

1. Sidecar recipe	2. Guacamole recipe (first few steps)
A. Coat the rim of a cocktail glass with sugar and set aside. B. Add the remaining ingredients to a shaker and fill with ice. C. Shake and strain into the prepared glass. D. Garnish with a piece of orange peel.	A. Cut open avocados and scoop them out. B. Discard skin and pits. C. Use a fork or mixer to blend the avocados until smooth D. ...

Figure 1: Example recipes. Left: for a mixed drink. Right: for guacamole dip.

2 Challenges

This section surveys some of the linguistic challenges typical of the cooking domain, as illustrated by the two recipes in Figure 1. These difficulties can be classified broadly as problems arising from the interpretation of **arguments**, **actions** and **control structure**.

Arguments: One particularly salient characteristic of recipes is that they often feature arguments that are omitted, underspecified or otherwise dependent on the context. Arguments may be *elided* in syntactic contexts where they are usually required (the so-called "zero anaphora" problem), especially when they are easily filled by an object in the immediate context. For example, the item to set aside in (1a) is the just-treated cocktail glass, and the item to fill in (1b) and shake and then strain in (1c) is the recently mentioned shaker. Note that the context may include the ingredient list itself, as illustrated by the elided argument(s) to be added in the one-line recipe "Add to a cocktail glass in the order listed." Arguments may be *implicitly available*, based on either domain-specific expectations of the initial context or the results of pre-

[1] http://www.google.com/insidesearch/features/recipes/

[2] See e.g. http://microformats.org/wiki/recipe-formats

Proceedings of the ACL 2014 Workshop on Semantic Parsing, pages 33–38,
Baltimore, Maryland USA, June 26 2014.

ceding steps. The ice in (1b) isn't listed in the corresponding recipes ingredient list, since many common ingredients (water, ice, salt, pepper) are assumed to be available in most kitchens. Sometimes, the argument may never have been directly verbalized, but rather is the result of a previous action. Thus in the recipe "Pour ingredients over ice and shake vigorously," the object to shake is the container (only implicitly available) along with its contents — which, once the "pour" instruction is executed, include both ice and the (listed) ingredients. Note also that interpreting "the remaining ingredients" in (1b) requires an understanding of which ingredients have yet to be used at that point in the recipe. Arguments may be *indirectly available*, by association with an explicitly available argument. Recipe 2 mentions avocados in several explicit and implicit referring expressions; of these only the "them" in (2a) may be considered straightforward anaphoric reference (to the just-cut avocados). Step (2b) involves a metonymic reference to the "skin and pits" where the part-whole relation between these items and the avocado is what makes the instruction interpretable. Step (2c) once again mentions "avocados", but note that this now refers to the flesh of the avocados, i.e., the implicit scooped-out object from (2a). Arguments may be *incompletely specified*, especially with respect to amount. The exact amount of sugar needed in (1a) is not mentioned, for example. Similarly, the amount of ice needed in (1b) depends on the size of the shaker and is not precisely specified.

Actions: Like arguments, action interpretation also depends on the situational context. For example, actions may have *ambiguous senses*, mainly due to the elided arguments noted above. The verb "shake" in (1c), for example, yields a spurious intransitive reading. Actions may have *argument-dependent senses*: certain verbs may resolve to different motor actions depending on the affordances of their arguments. For example, the action intended by the verb "garnish" in (1d) might involve careful perching of the peel on the rim of the glass; in other recipes, the same verb applied to nutmeg or cut fruit may be better interpreted as an add action. Actions may be *omitted* or *implied*, in particular by the way certain arguments are expressed. Most recipes involving eggs, for example, do not explicitly mention the need to crack them and extract their contents; this is a default preparatory step. Other ingredients vary in how strongly they are associated with (implicit) preparatory steps. For example, recipes calling for "1/4 avocado" may require that something like steps (2a-b) be undertaken (and their results quartered); the "orange peel" of (1d) may likewise depend on a separate procedure for extracting peel from an orange.

Control structure: Instructions sometimes provide more complex information about sequence, coordination and control conditions. **Conditions**: An action may be specified as being performed until some finish condition holds. In (2c), the "until smooth" condition—itself featuring an elided avocado argument—controls how long the blending action should continue. Other conditions mentioned in recipes include "Add crushed ice until the glass is almost full", "Stir until the glass begins to frost", and "Add salt to taste". **Sequence**: Though implicitly sequential, recipes occasionally include explicit sequencing language. In the recipe "Add to a cocktail glass in the order listed", the order reflects that of the ingredient list. Other recipes specify that certain steps can or should be done "ahead of time", or else while other steps are in progress. **Alternatives**: Recipes sometimes allow for some variability, by specifying alternative options for specific ingredients ("Garnish with a twist of lemon or lime"), appliances or utensils ("Using a large fork (or a blender)..."), and even actions ("Chop or mash the avocados").

As should be clear from these examples, the interpretation of a given step in a set of instructions may hinge on many aspects of situated and procedural knowledge, including at least: the physical context (including the particular props and tools assumed available); the incremental state resulting from successful execution of previous steps; and general commonsense knowledge about the affordances of specific objects or expected arguments of specific actions (or more conveniently, corpus-based verb-argument expectations that approximate such knowledge, see e.g., (Nyga and Beetz, 2012)). All of these sources of knowledge go significantly beyond those employed in semantic parsing models for single utterances and in non-procedural contexts.

3 Proposed approach

We propose to maintain a rich latent context that persists while parsing an entire recipe, in contrast

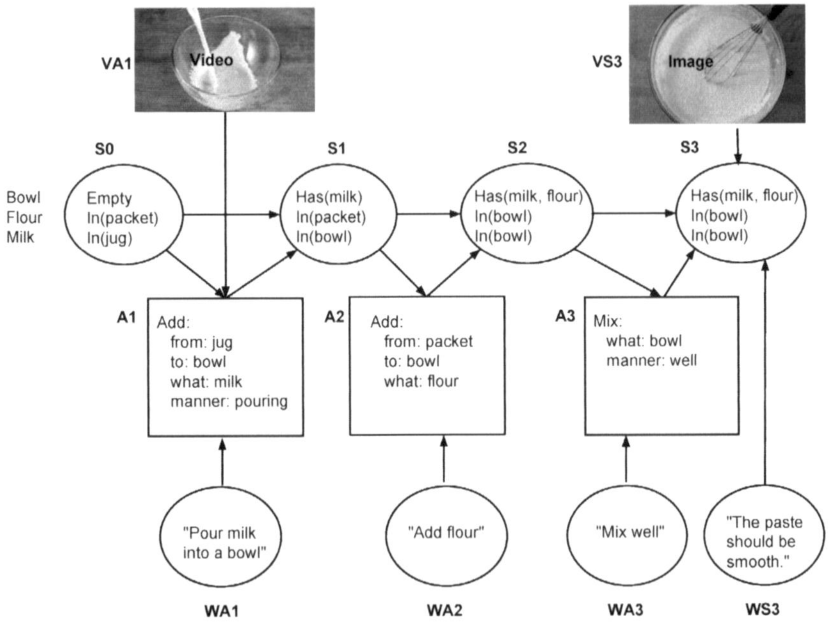

Figure 2: Our proposed probabilistic model, showing a possible trace of observed and latent variables after parsing each step of a pancake recipe. See text for description of notation.

to approaches that interpret each sentence independently. This context represents the state of the kitchen, and statements in the recipes are interpreted pragmatically with respect to the evolving context. More precisely, our model has the overall structure of a discrete-time, partially observed, object-oriented Markov Decision Process, as illustrated in Figure 2. The states and actions are both hidden. What we observe is text and/or images/video; our goal is to infer the posterior over the sequence of actions (i.e., to recover the "true" recipe), given the noisy evidence.

States and actions. The world state S_t is represented as a set of objects, such as ingredients and containers, along with various predicates, encoding the quantity, location, and condition (e.g., raw or cooked, empty or full) of each object. Note that previous work on situated semantic parsing often uses grid world environments where the only fluent is the agent's location; in contrast, we allow any object to undergo state transformations. In particular, objects can be created and destroyed.

Each action A_t is represented by a *semantic frame*, corresponding to a verb with various arguments or roles. This specifies how to transform the state. We also allow for sequencing and loop frames c.f., the "robot control language" in (Matuszek et al., 2013). We assume access to a simple cooking simulator that can take in a stream of low-level instructions to produce a new state; this implements the world dynamics model $p(S_t|S_{t-1}, A_t)$.

Text data. We assume that the text of the t'th sentence, represented by WA_t, describes the t'th primitive action, A_t. We represent the conditional distribution $p(A_t|WA_t, S_{t-1})$ as a log-linear model, as in prior work on frame-semantic parsing/ semantic role labeling (SRL) (Das et al., 2014).[3] However, we extend this prior work by allowing roles to be filled not just from spans from the text, but also by objects in the latent state vector. We will use various pragmatically-inspired features to represent the compatibility between candidate objects in the state vector and roles in the action frame, including: whether the object has been recently mentioned or touched, whether the object has the right affordances for the corresponding role (e.g., if the frame is "mix", and the role is "what", the object should be mixable),

[3]Although CCGs have been used in previous work on (situated) semantic parsing, such as (Artzi and Zettlemoyer, 2013), we chose to use the simpler approach based on frames because the nature of the language that occurs in recipes is sufficiently simple (there are very few complex nested clauses).

etc. More sophisticated models, based on modeling the belief state of the listener (e.g., (Goodman and Stuhlmüller, 2013; Vogel et al., 2013)) are also possible and within the scope of future work.

In addition to imperative sentences, we sometimes encounter descriptive sentences that describe what the state should look like at a given step (c.f., (Lau et al., 2009)). We let WS_t denote a sentence (possibly empty) describing the t'th state, S_t. The distribution $p(\mathrm{S}_t|\mathrm{WS}_t)$ is a discriminative probabilistic classifier of some form.

Visual data. Much instructional information is available in the form of how-to videos. In addition, some textual instructions are accompanied by static images. We would like to extend the model to exploit such data, when available.

Let a video clip associated with an action at time t be denoted by VA_t. We propose to learn $p(\mathrm{A}_t|\mathrm{VA}_t)$ using supervised machine learning. For features, we could use the output of standard object detectors and their temporal trajectories, as in (Yu and Siskind, 2013), bags of visual words derived from temporal HOG descriptors as in (Das et al., 2013), or features derived from RGB-D sensors such as Kinect, as in (Song et al., 2013; Lei et al., 2012).

There are many possible ways to fuse the information from vision and text, i.e., to compute $p(\mathrm{A}_t|\mathrm{VA}_t, \mathrm{WA}_t, \mathrm{S}_{t-1})$. The simplest approach is to separately train the two conditionals, $p(\mathrm{A}_t|\mathrm{WA}_t, \mathrm{S}_{t-1})$ and $p(\mathrm{A}_t|\mathrm{VA}_t)$, and then train another model to combine them, using a separate validation set; this will learn the relative reliability of the two sources of signal.

Learning and inference. We assume that we have manually labeled the actions A_t, and that the initial state S_0 is fully observed (e.g., a list of ingredients, with all containers empty). If we additional assume that the world dynamics model is known[4] and deterministic, then we can uniquely infer the sequence of states $\mathrm{S}_{1:T}$. This lets us use standard supervised learning to fit the log-linear model $p(\mathrm{A}_t|\mathrm{WA}_t, \mathrm{S}_{t-1})$.

In the future, we plan to relax the assumption of fully labeled training data, and to allow for learning from a distant supervision signal, similar to (Artzi and Zettlemoyer, 2013; Branavan et al., 2009). For example, we can prefer a parse that results in a final state in which all the ingredients have been consumed, and the meal is prepared.

[4]There has been prior work on learning world models from text, see e.g., (Sil and Yates, 2011; Branavan et al., 2012).

4 Preliminary results

We conducted a preliminary analysis to gauge the feasibility and expected performance benefits of our approach. We used the raw recipes provided in the CMU Recipe Database (Tasse and Smith, 2008), which consists of 260 English recipes downloaded from `allrecipes.com`. We then applied a state-of-the art SRL system (Das et al., 2014) to the corpus, using Propbank (Palmer et al., 2005) as our frame repository. Figure 3 summarizes our findings.

To judge the variance of predicates used in the cooking domain, we computed the frequency of each word tagged as a present-tense verb by a statistical part-of-speech tagger, filtering out a small number of common auxiliary verbs. Our findings suggest a relatively small number of verbs account for a large percentage of observed instructions (e.g, "add", "bake", and "stir"). The majority of these verbs have corresponding framesets that are usually correctly recognized, with some notable exceptions. Further, the most common observed framesets have a straightforward mapping to our set of kitchen state transformations, such as object creation via combination ("add", "mix", "combine", "stir in"), location transfers ("place", "set"), and discrete state changes over a small space of features ("cook", "cut", "cool", "bake").

To gain a preliminary understand of the limitations of the current SRL system and the possible performance benefits of our proposed system, we hand-annotated five of our recipes as follows: Each verb in the recipe corresponding to an action was annotated with its best corresponding roleset (if any). Each role in that roleset was marked as either being explicitly present in the text, implicitly present in our latent kitchen model but not in the text (and so in principle, fillable by our model), or neither present in the text nor in our model. For example, in"cover for forty minutes", the frameset "cover" has an explicit temporal role-filling ("for forty minutes") and an implicit role-filling ("the pot" as the patient of "cover").

For each verb in the annotation, we checked if the SRL system mapped that verb to the correct roleset and if so, whether it filled the same semantic roles as the annotator indicated were explicitly present in the text. Overall, we found 54% recall of the annotations by the SRL system. We quali-

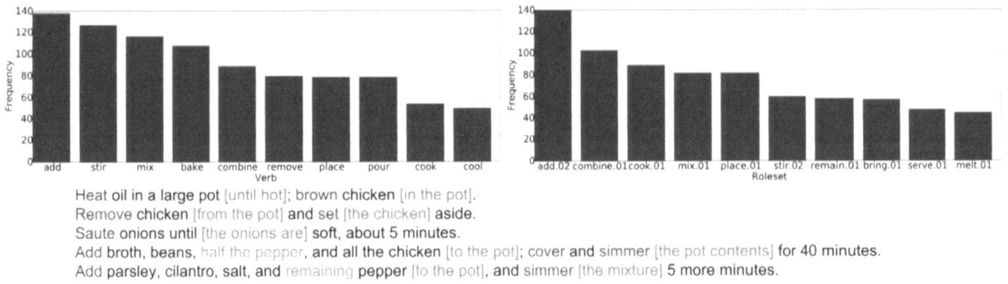

Figure 3: Results. Top: Distribution of the ten most common verbs and framesets in 260 recipes from allrecipes.com. Bottom: An example recipe annotation. Blue indicates propbank predicates. Bracketed red indicates implicit propbank arguments not in the text, but in principle recognizable by our model. Green indicates quantifier adjectives which our model could resolve to an exact quantity, given initial ingredient amounts.

tatively notes several failure modes. Many errors arise from not recognizing predicates represented in the text as an imperative verb, likely because PropBank contains few examples of such language for the labeler to learn from. Other errors result from ungrammatical constructs (e.g. in "cook five minutes", the eliding of "for" causes "five minutes" to incorrectly parse as a direct argument). Certain cooking-related verbs lack framesets entirely, such as "prebake". Occasionally, the wrong roleset is chosen. For example, in"Stir the mixture" , "Stir" is labeled as "stir.02: cause (emotional) reaction" rather than "stir.01: mix with a circular motion".

We also analyzed the quantity and qualitative trends in the human annotations that refer to roles fillable from the latent kitchen model but not literally present in the text. Overall, 52% of verb annotations referenced at least one such role. The most common situation (occurring for 36% of all annotated verbs) is the "patient/direct object" role is elided in the text but inferable from the world state, as in "simmer [the mixture] for 40 minutes". The second most common is the "location" modifier role is elided in the text, as in "Remove chicken [from the pot]". Overall, we believe our proposed approach will improve the quality of the SRL system, and thus the overall interpretability of the recipes.

5 Possible applications

We believe that semantic parsing of recipes and other instructional text could support a rich array of applications, such as the following:

Deriving a "canonical" recipe. It would be useful to align different versions of the same recipe to derive a "canonical form" cf., (Druck and Pang, 2012; Tenorth et al., 2013b).

Explaining individual steps. It would be helpful if a user could click on a confusing step in a recipe and get a more detailed explanation and/or an illustrative video clip.

Automatically interpreting software instructions. Going beyond the recipe domain, it would be useful to develop a system which can interpret instructions such as how to install software, and then automatically execute them (i.e., install the software for you). In practice, this may be too hard, so we could allow the system to ask for human help if it gets stuck, cf. (Deits et al., 2013).

Robotics. (Tenorth et al., 2013a) suggest mining natural language "action recipes" as a way to specify tasks for service robots. In the domain of food recipes, there have already been several demonstrations (e.g., (Beetz et al., 2011; Bollini et al., 2013)) of robots automatically cooking meals based on recipes.

Task assistance using augmented reality. Imagine tracking the user as they follow some instructions using a device such as Google glass, and offering help when needed. Such systems have been developed before for specialized domains like maintenance and repair of military hardware[5], but automatic parsing of natural language text potentially opens this up to the consumer market. (Note that there is already a recipe app for Google Glass[6], although it just displays a static list of instructions.)

[5]For example, see `http://graphics.cs.columbia.edu/projects/armar/index.htm`.

[6]See `http://www.glassappsource.com/listing/all-the-cooks-recipes`.

References

Y. Artzi and L. Zettlemoyer. 2013. Weakly supervised learning of semantic parsers for mapping instructions to actions. *Trans. Assoc. for Computational Linguistics*, 1:49–62.

M. Beetz, U. Klank, I. Kreese, A. Maldonado, L. Mosenlechner, D. Pangercic, T. Ruhr, and M. Tenorth. 2011. Robotic roommates making pancakes. In *Intl. Conf. on Humanoid Robots*.

Mario Bollini, Stefanie Tellex, Tyler Thompson, Nicholas Roy, and Daniela Rus. 2013. Interpreting and executing recipes with a cooking robot. *Experimental Robotics*.

SRK Branavan, H. Chen, L. Zettlemoyer, and R. Barzilay. 2009. Reinforcement learning for mapping instructions to actions. In *Association for Computational Linguistics*.

S.R.K. Branavan, N. Kushman, T. Lei, and R. Barzilay. 2012. Learning High-Level Planning from Text. In *ACL*.

P. Das, C. Xu, R. F. Doell, and J. J. Corso. 2013. A thousand frames in just a few words: Lingual description of videos through latent topics and sparse object stitching. In *CVPR*.

D. Das, D. Chen, A. Martins, N. Schneider, and N. Smith. 2014. Frame-semantic parsing. *Computational Linguistics*.

R. Deits, S. Tellex, P. Thaker, D. Simeonov, T. Kollar, and N. Roy. 2013. Clarifying Commands with Information-Theoretic Human-Robot Dialog. *J. Human-Robot Interaction*.

G. Druck and B. Pang. 2012. Spice it Up? Mining Renements to Online Instructions from User Generated Content. In *ACL*.

Noah D Goodman and Andreas Stuhlmüller. 2013. Knowledge and implicature: Modeling language understanding as social cognition. *Topics in cognitive science*, 5(1):173–184.

TA Lau, Clemens Drews, and Jeffrey Nichols. 2009. Interpreting Written How-To Instructions. *IJCAI*.

J. Lei, X. Ren, and D. Fox. 2012. Fine-grained kitchen activity recognition using RGB-D. In *Ubicomp*.

C. Matuszek, E. Herbst, L. Zettlemoyer, and D. Fox. 2013. Learning to parse natural language commands to a robot control system. *Experimental Robotics*, pages 1–14.

D. Nyga and M. Beetz. 2012. Everything robots always wanted to know about housework (but were afraid to ask). In *Intl. Conf. on Intelligent Robots and Systems*.

M. Palmer, D. Gildea, and P. Kingsbury. 2005. The proposition bank: An annotated corpus of semantic roles. *Computational Linguistics*, 31(1):71–106.

A. Sil and A. Yates. 2011. Extracting STRIPS Representations of Actions and Events. In *Recent Advances in NLP*.

Young Chol Song, Henry Kautz, James Allen, Mary Swift, Yuncheng Li, Jiebo Luo, and Ce Zhang. 2013. A markov logic framework for recognizing complex events from multimodal data. In *Proc. 15th ACM Intl. Conf. Multimodal Interaction*, pages 141–148. ACM.

D. Tasse and N. Smith. 2008. SOUR CREAM: Toward Semantic Processing of Recipes. Technical Report CMU-LTI-08-005, Carnegie Mellon University, Pittsburgh, PA.

M. Tenorth, A. Perzylo, R. Lafrenz, and M. Beetz. 2013a. Representation and exchange of knowledge about actions, objects, and environments in the roboearth framework. *IEEE Trans. on Automation Science and Engineering*, 10(3):643–651.

M. Tenorth, J. Ziegltrum, and M. Beetz. 2013b. Automated alignment of specifications of everyday manipulation tasks. In *IEEE Intl. Conf. on Intelligent Robots and Systems*.

A. Vogel, M. Bodoia, C. Potts, and D. Jurafsky. 2013. Emergence of Gricean Maxims from Multi-Agent Decision Theory. In *NAACL*.

Haonan Yu and JM Siskind. 2013. Grounded language learning from video described with sentences. In *Association for Computational Linguistics*.

Representing Caused Motion in Embodied Construction Grammar

Ellen K. Dodge
International Computer Science Institute
Berkeley, CA, USA 94704
edodge@icsi.berkeley.edu

Miriam R. L. Petruck
International Computer Science Institute
Berkeley, CA, USA 94704
miriamp@icsi.berkeley.edu

Abstract

This paper offers an Embodied Construction Grammar (Feldman et al. 2010) representation of caused motion, thereby also providing (a sample of) the computational infrastructure for implementing the information that FrameNet has characterized as `Caused_motion`[1] (Ruppenhofer et al. 2010). This work specifies the semantic structure of caused motion in natural language, using an Embodied Construction Grammar analyzer that includes the semantic parsing of linguistically instantiated constructions. Results from this type of analysis can serve as the input to NLP applications that require rich semantic representations.

1 Introduction

Computational linguistics recognizes the difficulty in articulating the nature of complex events, including causation, while understanding that doing so is fundamental for creating natural language processing (NLP) systems (e.g. Girju 2003, Quang et al. 2011), and more generally for other computational techniques (Guyon et al. 2007, Friedman et al. 2000). Also, although insightful, linguistic analyses of causation are insufficient for systems that require drawing the inferences that humans draw with ease. Such systems must incorporate information about the parameters that support drawing these inferences. Embodied Construction Grammar (ECG) provides the computational and representational apparatus for capturing what language expresses.

FrameNet (FN) frames capture event structure in terms of the participants that play a role in that event. ECG provides a means for the automatic identification of frames and frame roles expressed in any given sentence. Here, we focus on a pair of sentences that illustrate the rich meanings and relations characterized in FN frames as represented in ECG.

This paper is organized as follows: Section 2 includes background information on FrameNet (FN) and ECG; Section 3 describes the FN treatment of `Caused_motion`, and the ECG representation of the CauseMotion schema, which constitutes the meaning block of the Cause_motion construction; Section 4 summarizes the ECG analysis of motion and caused motion example sentences; and Section 5 discusses new directions for future work with ECG representations of information structured in FrameNet frames (http://framenet.icsi.berkeley.edu).

2 Background

Chang et al. (2002) constitutes the first effort to represent the prose description of the information that FN has defined in semantic frames in formal terms. The work provided an ECG representation of FN's (then) `Commerce` frame, showing the perspicuity of doing so to account for linguistic perspective, and ultimately useful in translating FN information into a representation needed for event simulation (Narayanan 1997). Building on Chang et al. (2002), this paper focuses on the analysis and representation of the meanings of sentences describing different kinds of motion events, using a set of related semantic frames. Before detailing the examples that illustrate the analysis and representation, we offer a very brief overview of FN and ECG.

2.1 FrameNet

The FrameNet knowledge base holds unique information on the mapping of meaning to form via the theory of Frame Semantics (Fillmore and Baker 2010), at the heart of which is the semantic frame, i.e. an experience-based schematization of the language user's world that allows inferences about participants and objects in and across situations, states of affairs, and events. FN

[1] `Courier New` font indicates a FrameNet frame; and small CAPS indicate a FE in a FN frame.

Proceedings of the ACL 2014 Workshop on Semantic Parsing, pages 39–44,
Baltimore, Maryland USA, June 26 2014.

has characterized nearly 1,200 frames, more than 12,740 lexical units (LUs), where a lexical unit is a pairing of a lemma and a frame, and approximately 200,000 manually annotated example sentences that illustrate usage of each LU.

A FN frame definition includes a prose description of a prototypical situation, along with a specification of the frame elements (FEs), or semantic roles, that uniquely characterize that situation. For example, FN has defined `Motion` as a situation in which a THEME starts out at a SOURCE, moves along a PATH, and ends up at a GOAL.[2] Example (1) illustrates FN's analysis of **SLIDE**, one of many LUs, in the `Motion` frame, also indicating which constituents in the sentence are the linguistic realizations of the FEs THEME and GOAL.

(1) [The envelope $_{\text{THEME}}$] **SLID** [into the mailbox $_{\text{GOAL}}$].

2.2 Embodied Construction Grammar

An ECG grammar (Feldman et al. 2010) consists of structured lattices of two basic primitives: **schemas** and **constructions**. As with other forms of construction grammar, a key tenet of ECG is that each construction is a form-meaning pair. Constructional meaning is represented using schemas, which are analogous to FN frames. Each schema includes several roles (comparable to FN's FEs), and specifies various types of constraints on its roles. Thus, the ECG formalism provides the means for representing frame structure and relations in a precise and computationally tractable manner.

Crucially, our computationally implemented system (Bryant 2008) uses an ECG grammar for sentence interpretation and produces construction-based semantic parses. The Constructional Analyzer utilizes **form and meaning** information in the constructional analysis of a given sentence. Thus, constructional analysis is not just a form match; importantly, it is a meaning match as well. The output of the analysis is a semantic specification, a meaning representation in the form of schemas, roles, bindings, and role-filler information. Constructional analysis is part of a larger model of language understanding, in which the semantic specification, in conjunction with discourse and situational context, serves as an input for a simulation process, which fleshes out and supports further inferences about the relatively schematic meaning specified in the text.

Among the potential applications for such deep semantic analysis are question-answering tasks, information extraction, and identifying different political viewpoints. Each task has its own requirements in terms of constructions and semantic representations. This paper illustrates a computationally implemented means for determining the frames and frame roles in a given sentence, as well as the particular entities that link to those roles.

Figure 1 shows the ECG formalism that represents the semantic structure of FN's `Motion` frame, where the MotionPath schema specifies the structural relationships among the participants (FEs) in FN's `Motion` frame.

```
schema MotionPath
  subcase of Motion
  evokes SPG as SPG
  roles
    mover
    landmark
    source
    path
    goal
  constraints
    mover <--> spg.trajector
```

Figure 1: MotionPath Schema

ECG defines MotionPath as a **subcase of** the very general Motion schema; as a child of the Motion schema, MotionPath inherits the structure of Motion, the latter including a mover role. Also, MotionPath **evokes** a Source-Path-Goal (SPG) schema, which includes the roles source, path, and goal, for the initial, medial, and final locations, respectively, of a trajector. MotionPath also includes a **constraint** that the mover is bound to the trajector role.

A construction is a pairing between form and meanng, the ECG representation of which consists of a **form** block and a **meaning** block. To illustrate, in Figure 2, which shows the simple lexical construction Slid_Past, the form block indicates the orthographic form associated with the lexical construction. The form constraint indicates that the constraint applies to the form of the construction (self.f.orth <-- "slid"), where .orth indicates that the form is a text string, in this case "slid". ECG represents constructional meaning using schemas; in the Slid_Past construction, (Figure 2), the meaning is identified with the MotionPath schema (as shown in Figure 1). Constructions also define relations to other

[2] FN also describes another scenario for `Motion`, not included here for space-saving reasons.

constructions in the grammar. For instance, Slid_Past is a subcase of a more general PastTense construction. The PastTense construction is one of several general verb conjugation constructions in the grammar, each of which captures general facts about tense and aspect associated with different verb conjugation forms. For example, all past tense verbs, including *slid* (an instantiation of Slid_Past), use PastTense.

```
construction SlidPast
subcase of Slide, PastTense
form
constraints
self.f.orth <-- "slid"
meaning: MotionPath
```

Figure 2: Slid_Past Construction

3 Caused_motion

This section describes FN's characterization of `Caused_motion` and provides the ECG representation of the CausedMotion schema, i.e., the meaning of the Cause_motion construction.

3.1 FrameNet

FrameNet characterizes `Caused_motion` as a situation in which an AGENT causes a THEME to undergo translation motion, where the motion also may always be described with respect to a SOURCE, PATH, and GOAL.[3] Example (2) shows the FN analysis with **SLIDE** as the target verb in `Caused_motion`, marking the constituents that fill the AGENT, THEME, and GOAL roles.

(2) [Smedlap $_{\text{AGENT}}$] **SLID** [the envelope $_{\text{THEME}}$] into the mailbox $_{\text{GOAL}}$].

Note that whereas FN's `Caused_motion` frame has an AGENT FE, `Motion` does not.

FrameNet Frame	Frame Elements	Example Sentence
`Motion`	THEME SOURCE PATH GOAL	The envelope slid into the mailbox.
`Caused_motion`	AGENT THEME SOURCE PATH GOAL	Smedlap slid the envelope into the mailbox.

Table 1: FN's `Motion` and `Caused_motion`

[3] As with `Motion`, FN also defines another scenario for `Caused_motion`, specifically one with a CAUSE FE, excluded here because of space limitations.

3.2 Embodied Construction Grammar

The ECG representation of CauseMotion, given in Figure 3, is a complex schema that combines the structure of causation with that of translational motion. The causal structure is supplied by defining CauseMotion as a subcase of a more general CauseEffect schema, which includes roles for a causal agent and an affected entity. Also, CauseMotion specifies that the effect is translational motion, indicated with the addition of a type constraint that identifies the effect with the MotionPath schema.

```
schema CauseMotion
  subcase of CauseEffect
  roles
    causalProcess
    effect: MotionPath
    causer
    affected
```

Figure 3: CauseMotion Schema

Additional constraints bind the mover role of MotionPath (Figure 1) to the affected role of CauseMotion. Thus, the ECG mover (i.e. the FE THEME) is bound to the affected role; and the motion itself is bound to the effect. ECG uses the CauseMotion schema to analyze sentences such as Example (2), an instance of the Cause_motion construction, a summary of which follows below in Section 4.

4 ECG for Linguistic Analysis

Here, we provide an overview of the ECG analysis process for the examples discussed above.

A basic tenet of construction grammar is that each sentence instantiates multiple constructions. Bryant's (2008) computationally implemented Constructional Analyzer uses an ECG grammar to determine the set of constructions that best-fit a given sentence.[4] The assessment of "best-fit" takes both syntactic and semantic information into account. Constructional unification requires compatibility between unifying elements. Unification tests the compatibility of the constraints that these constructions specify, and leads to various bindings. The analyzer produces a SemSpec, i.e. a semantic specification of the sentence, that is, a meaning representation in the form of a network of schemas, with bindings between schema roles and fillers of these roles.

[4] ECG Workbench provides an interface to the analyzer, and allows the viewing of analysis results.

To illustrate the analysis process, we revisit Example (1) *The envelope slid into the mailbox*, which instantiates some of the following lexical and grammatical constructions:

- Lexical constructions for *slid*, nouns (*envelope, mailbox*), and determiners (*the*)
- NP constructions (*the envelope*, *the mailbox*)
- Declarative construction, a clause-level construction spanning the sentence as a whole.

In what follows, we define and explain the constructions in Example (1) that are crucial for the present analysis of Motion and CausedMotion. Specifically, the Active_Motion_Path construction (Figure 4) is a sub-case of a more general Argument Structure construction (Goldberg 1995, Dodge 2010). Argument Structure (A-S) constructions specify general patterns of role expression associated with the description of basic experiences, such as those involving motion, perception, object transfer, actions and/or causation. Schemas represent each type of experience and include roles for the relevant participant(s). A-S constructions include one or more constituent constructions, specified within their **constructional** block. All A-S constructions include a verb constituent (V: Verb); here, note that the Active_Motion_Path construction also contains a prepositional phrase constituent (PP), constrained to be of type Path-PP, a general construction that identifies its meaning with the SPG schema. The form block specifies ordering constraints: the V constituent comes before the PP constituent. The meaning block specifies that the construction's meaning is identified with the MotionPath schema, indicating that the construction describes translational motion events. Constraints within the meaning block specify how the meaning of the construction as a whole composes with the meanings of its constituents. As is usually the case, the 'V' constituent shares the same schematic meaning as the A-S construction. These constraints indicate that the A-S construction will unify with verbs that identify their meaning with the MotionPath schema, as in the motion verbs *roll, slip*, *bounce*, etc, along with *slide*. Thus, this A-S construction captures a particular valence pattern associated with several semantically similar verbs.

A further meaning constraint indicates that the meaning of the PP constituent serves to elaborate the SPG schema that forms part of the meaning of the MotionPath schema. That is, whichever specific PP serves as a constituent in a given example will supply more information about the particular path of motion the mover is following. Additionally, the mover role of MotionPath is bound to the profiledParticipant role (i.e., the semantic correlate of the role expressed in the sentence's subject slot), and the meaning of the construction as a whole binds to an eventProcess role, which indicates the type of event that this A-S construction describes.

```
construction ActiveMotionPath
 subcase of ArgumentStructure
 constructional
  constituents
   v: Verb
   pp: Path-PP
 form
  constraints
   v.f before pp.f
 meaning: MotionPath
  constraints
   self.m <--> v.m
   self.m.spg <--> pp.m
   self.m.mover <--> ed.profiledParticipant
  self.m <--> ed.eventProcess
```

Figure 4: Active_Motion_Path Construction

Constraint-based unification of the instantiated construction produces a SemSpec that includes the following information: (1) a MotionPath schema is co-indexed with the 'eventProcess' role, indicating that the sentence describes an event of translational motion; (2) the meaning of *the envelope* is co-indexed with the profiledParticipant role, the mover of MotionPath, and the trajector of SPG, indicating that this object is the semantic subject of the sentence, and that it is the entity that moves and changes location with respect to a landmark; and (3) the meaning of *the mailbox* is co-indexed with the landmark of SPG, and the boundedObject role of a BoundedObject schema. The source of SPG is bound to the exterior role of boundedObject. The goal of SPG is bound to the interior of boundedObject. Together, these bindings indicate that the mailbox is conceptualized as a bounded object or container, the envelope's initial location (source) is outside of the mailbox, and its final location is inside.

Having analyzed a sentence about motion, we return to our example of caused motion: (2) *Smedlap slid the envelope into the mailbox*. This sentence instantiates many of the same constructions as does Example (1). The key difference between the two is the A-S construction, here the

Active_Transitive_Caused_Motion construction, shown below in Figure 5.

```
construction ActiveTransitiveCausedMotion
  subcase of ActiveTransitive
   constructional
     constituents
       V: Verb
       np: NP
       pp: Path-PP
   form
    constraints
       v.f before np.f
       np.f before pp.f
   meaning: CauseMotion
    constraints
       v.m <-->self.m.process2
       self.m.causer <--> ed.profiledParticipant
       np.m <--> self.m.affected
       self.m.spg <--> pp.m
```

Figure 5:Active_Transitive_Caused_Motion

This is similar to the Active_Motion_Path construction in that it has both a V and a PP constituent. However, as with other A-S constructions that characterize transitives, this A-S construction also includes an NP constituent, whose form follows that of the verb. Crucially, this A-S construction identifies its meaning with CauseMotion, indicating that it is used to describe scenes which a causal agent causes the translational motion of some other entity. Meaning constraints specify that the affected role of CauseMotion is bound to the meaning of the NP constituent, and the causer role is bound to the profiled participant role. This latter constraint indicates that this active voice construction describes caused motion events from the causer's perspective.

Using these constructions, the analysis of Example (2) produces a SemSpec that is similar to that produced for Example (1), with the following key differences:

- the eventProcess is CausedMotion (rather than MotionPath);
- the profiledParticipant role is bound to the causer role of CauseMotion, and to *Smedlap*;
- *the envelope* is bound to the affected role of CauseMotion, as well as to the mover role of MotionPath, and the trajector role of SPG.

This SemSpec for Example (2) indicates that:

- the sentence describes an event of caused motion, represented by the CauseMotion schema;
- the caused effect is motion, represented by the MotionPath schema;
- the subject (*Smedlap*) is the causer of the motion;
- the direct object (*the envelope*) is the causally affected entity that moves.
- the path of motion is one where with the goal location inside the entity that the prepositional phrase object (*the mailbox*) specifies, just as in Example (1).

To summarize, the semantic representation output of the ECG analysis process for each of Examples (1) and (2) identifies that they evoke the MotionPath and CauseMotion schemas, respectively (analogous to FN's `Motion` and `Cause_Motion`, respectively). Also, the output specifies the different roles (FEs) that the different constituents of each sentence realize. Thus, the information provided by such output identifies the frames and frame roles expressed in each sentence.

5 Extensions

Given the compositional nature of the ECG grammar, it will also support the analysis of other sentences describing translational motion and caused motion events that differ in terms of the lexical items that are realized. Consider the following new examples.

- His hat is slipping off his head.
- Did the dog roll the ball under the table?
- Which leaf fell off the tree?

Moreover, the approach outlined here clearly also would apply to the analysis of all FrameNet frames that characterize, for instance, cognition, perception, communication or other causal events or transitive actions.

Research has begun to extend the present work to support the analysis of metaphorical uses of motion and caused motion frame structure, as in: *The young family slid into poverty* or *Their huge debts dragged the young family into poverty.* This research requires the specification of appropriate constraints on the fillers of the roles that will facilitate distinguishing between the literal and the metaphorical.

References

J. Bryant. 2008. Best-Fit Constructional Analysis. Ph.D. Thesis, University of California, Berkeley.

N. Chang, S. Narayanan, M. R. L. Petruck. 2002. Putting frames in perspective, *Proc. of the 19th COLING, International Conference on Computational Linguistics*. Taipei, Taiwan.

E. K. Dodge. 2010.Constructional and Conceptual Composition Ph.D. Thesis, University of California, Berkeley.

J. Feldman, E. Dodge, J. Bryant. 2010. Embodied Construction Grammar. In B. Heine and H. Narrog (eds.), *The Oxford Handbook of Linguistic Analysis*, Oxford: Oxford University Press, pp. 111-158.

A. Goldberg. 1995. Constructions: *A Construction Grammar Approach to Argument Structure*. Chicago: University of Chicago Press.

N. Friedman, M. Linial, I. Nachman and D. Pe'er. 2000. Using Bayesian networks to analyze expression data. *Journal of Computational Biology* 7.3-4: 601-620.

R. Girju. 2003. Automatic detection of causal relations for question answering, *Proceedings of the ACL Workshop on Multilingual Summarization and Question Answering*: 76-83.

I. Guyon, A. Elisseeff and C. Aliferis. 2007. Causal feature selection, *Computational Methods of Feature Selection Data Mining and Knowledge Discovery Series*. Chapman and Hall/CRC, Boca Raton, London, New York, pp. 63-85.

S. Narayanan. 1997. Knowledge-based Action Representations for Metaphor and Aspect (KARMA). Ph.D. Thesis, University of California, Berkeley.

Q. Do, Y. Chan, and D. Roth. 2011. Minimally supervised event causality identification, *Proceedings of Empirical Methods in Natural Language Processing* (EMNLP), Edinburgh, Scotland, UK.

J. Ruppenhofer, M. Ellsworth, M. R. L. Petruck, C. R. Johnson, and J. Scheffczyk. 2010. *FrameNet II: Extended Theory and Practice* (Web Publication available via http://framenet.icsi.berkeley.edu).

Low-Dimensional Embeddings of Logic

Tim Rocktäschel[§] **Matko Bosnjak**[§] **Sameer Singh**[†] **Sebastian Riedel**[§]
[§]Department of Computer Science, University College London, UK
[†]Computer Science & Engineering, University of Washington, Seattle
{t.rocktaschel,m.bosnjak,s.riedel}@cs.ucl.ac.uk, sameer@cs.washington.edu

Abstract

Many machine reading approaches, from shallow information extraction to deep semantic parsing, map natural language to symbolic representations of meaning. Representations such as first-order logic capture the richness of natural language and support complex reasoning, but often fail in practice due to their reliance on logical background knowledge and the difficulty of scaling up inference. In contrast, low-dimensional embeddings (*i.e.* distributional representations) are efficient and enable generalization, but it is unclear how reasoning with embeddings could support the full power of symbolic representations such as first-order logic. In this proof-of-concept paper we address this by learning embeddings that simulate the behavior of first-order logic.

1 Introduction

Much of the work in machine reading follows an approach that is, at its heart, symbolic: language is transformed, possibly in a probabilistic way, into a symbolic world model such as a relational database or a knowledge base of first-order formulae. For example, a statistical relation extractor reads texts and populates relational tables (Mintz et al., 2009). Likewise, a semantic parser can turn sentences into complex first-order logic statements (Zettlemoyer and Collins, 2005).

Several properties make symbolic representations of knowledge attractive as a target of machine reading. They support a range of well understood symbolic reasoning processes, capture semantic concepts such as determiners, negations and tense, can be interpreted, edited and curated by humans to inject prior knowledge. However, on practical applications fully symbolic approaches have often shown low recall (*e.g.* Bos and Markert, 2005) as they are affected by the limited coverage of ontologies such as WordNet. Moreover, due to their deterministic nature they often cannot cope with noise and uncertainty inherent to real world data, and inference with such representations is difficult to scale up.

Embedding-based approaches address some of the concerns above. Here relational worlds are described using low-dimensional embeddings of entities and relations based on relational evidence in knowledge bases (Bordes et al., 2011) or surface-form relationships mentioned in text (Riedel et al., 2013). To overcome the generalization bottleneck, these approaches learn to embed similar entities and relations as vectors close in distance. Subsequently, unseen facts can be inferred by simple and efficient linear algebra operations (*e.g.* dot products).

The core argument against embeddings is their supposed inability to capture deeper semantics, and more complex patterns of reasoning such as those enabled by first-order logic (Lewis and Steedman, 2013). Here we argue that this does not need to be true. We present an approach that enables us to learn low-dimensional embeddings such that the model behaves *as if* it follows a complex first-order reasoning process—but still operates in terms of simple vector and matrix representations. In this view, machine reading becomes the process of taking (inherently symbolic) knowledge in language and injecting this knowledge into a sub-symbolic distributional world model. For example, one could envision a semantic parser that turns a sentence into a first-order logic statement,

Proceedings of the ACL 2014 Workshop on Semantic Parsing, pages 45–49,
Baltimore, Maryland USA, June 26 2014. ©2014 Association for Computational Linguistics

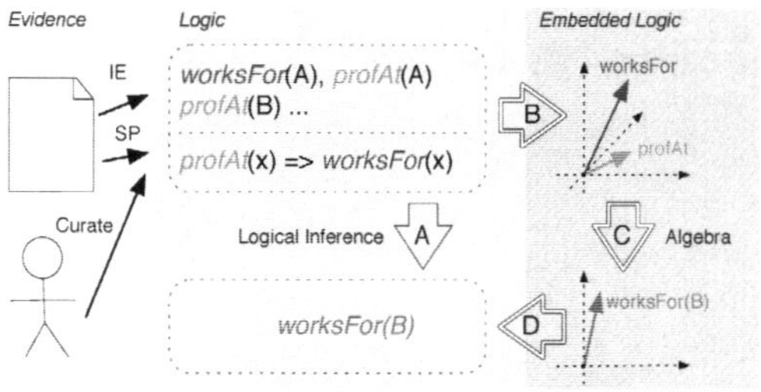

Figure 1: Information extraction (IE) and semantic parsing (SP) extract factual and more general logical statements from text, respectively. Humans can manually curate this knowledge. Instead of reasoning with this knowledge directly (A) we inject it into low dimensional representations of entities and relations (B). Linear algebra operations manipulate embeddings to derive truth vectors (C), which can be discretized or thresholded to retrieve truth values (D).

just to then inject this statement into the embeddings of relations and entities mentioned in the sentence.

2 Background

Figure 1 shows our problem setup. We assume a domain of a set of entities, such as SMITH and CAMBRIDGE, and relations among these (*e.g.* $\mathit{profAt}(\cdot,\cdot)$). We start from a knowledge base of observed logical statements, *e.g.*, $\mathit{profAt}(\text{SMITH}, \text{CAMBRIDGE})$ or $\forall x, y : \mathit{profAt}(x, y) \implies \mathit{worksFor}(x, y)$. These statements can be extracted from text through information extraction (for factual statements), be the output from a semantic parsing (for first-order statements) or come from human curators or external knowledge bases.

The task at hand is to predict the truth value of unseen statements, for example $\mathit{worksFor}(\text{SMITH}, \text{CAMBRIDGE})$. Assuming we have the corresponding formulae, logical inference can be used to arrive at this statement (arrow A in Figure 1). However, in practice the relevant background knowledge is usually missing. By contrast, a range of work (*e.g.* Bordes et al., 2011; Riedel et al., 2013) has successfully predicted unseen *factual* statements by learning entity and relation embeddings that recover the observed facts and generalize to unseen facts through dimensionality reduction (B). Inference in these approaches amounts to a series of algebraic operations on the learned embeddings that returns a numeric representation of the degree of truth (C), which can be thresholded to arrive back at a true or false statement (D) if needed.

Our goal in this view is to generalize (B) to allow richer logical statements to be recovered by low-dimensional embeddings. To this end we first describe how richer logical statements can be embedded at *full* dimension where the number of dimensions equals to the number of entities in the domain.

2.1 Tensor Calculus

Grefenstette (2013) presents an isomorphism between statements in predicate logic and expressions in tensor calculus. Let $[\cdot]$ denote this mapping from a logical expression $\mathcal{F}$ to an expression in tensor algebra. Here, logical statements evaluating to `true` or `false` are mapped to $[\texttt{true}] := \top = \begin{bmatrix}1 & 0\end{bmatrix}^T$ and $[\texttt{false}] := \bot = \begin{bmatrix}0 & 1\end{bmatrix}^T$ respectively.

Entities are represented by logical constants and mapped to one-hot vectors where each component represents a unique entity. For example, let $k = 3$ be the number of entities in a domain, then SMITH may be mapped to $[\text{SMITH}] = \begin{bmatrix}1 & 0 & 0\end{bmatrix}^T$. Unary predicates are represented as $2 \times k$ matrices, whose columns are composed of $\top$ and $\bot$ vectors. For example, for a *isProfessor* predicate we may get

$$[\mathit{isProfessor}] = \begin{bmatrix}1 & 0 & 1\\ 0 & 1 & 0\end{bmatrix}.$$

In this paper we treat binary relations as unary predicates over constants $\langle \text{X}, \text{Y} \rangle$ that correspond to pairs of entities X and Y in the domain.[1]

The application of a unary predicate to a constant is realized through matrix-vector multiplication. For example, for profAt and the entity pair $\langle \text{X}, \text{Y} \rangle$ we get

$$[\mathit{profAt}(\langle \text{X}, \text{Y} \rangle)] = [\mathit{profAt}]\,[\langle \text{X}, \text{Y} \rangle].$$

In Grefenstette's calculus, binary boolean operators are mapped to mode 3 tensors. For example, for the implication operator holds:

$$[\implies] := \left[\begin{array}{cc|cc}1 & 0 & 1 & 1\\ 0 & 1 & 0 & 0\end{array}\right].$$

Let A and B be two logical statements that, when evaluated in tensor algebra, yield a vector

[1]This simplifies our exposition and approach, and it can be shown that both representations are logically equivalent.

in $\{\top, \perp\}$. The application of a binary operator to statements A and B is realized via two consecutive tensor-vector products in their respective modes (see Kolda and Bader (2009) for details), *e.g.*,

$$[A \implies B] := [\implies] \times_1 [A] \times_2 [B] .$$

3 Method

Grefenstette's mapping to tensors exactly recovers the behavior of predicate logic. However, it also inherits the lack of generalization that comes with a purely symbolic representation. To overcome this problem we propose an alternate mapping. We retain the representation of truth values and boolean operators as the 2×1 and the $2 \times 2 \times 2$ sized tensors respectively. However, instead of mapping entities and predicates to one-hot representations, we estimate low-dimensional embeddings that recover the behavior of their one-hot counterparts when plugged into a set of tensor-logic statements.

In the following we first present a general learning objective that encourages low-dimensional embeddings to behave like one-hot representations. Then we show how this objective can be optimized for facts and implications.

3.1 Objective

Let $\mathfrak{R}$ be the set of all relation embeddings and $\mathfrak{P}$ be the set of all entity pair embeddings. Given a knowledge base (KB) of logical formulae K which we assume to hold, the objective is

$$\min_{[p]\in\mathfrak{P},\,[R]\in\mathfrak{R}} \sum_{\mathcal{F}\in K} \|[\mathcal{F}] - \top\|_2 . \qquad (1)$$

That is, we prefer embeddings for which the given formulae evaluate to the vector representation for truth. The same can be done for negative data by working with $\perp$, but we omit details for brevity.

To optimize this function we require the gradients of $\|[\mathcal{F}] - \top\|_2$ terms. Below we discuss these for two types of formulae: ground atoms and first-order formulae.

3.2 Ground Atoms

The KB may contain ground atoms (*i.e.* facts) of the form $\mathcal{F} = R(p)$ for a pair of entities p and a relation R. These atoms correspond to observed cells in an entity-pair-relation matrix, and injecting these facts into the embedding roughly corresponds to matrix factorization for link prediction or relation extraction (Riedel et al., 2013).

Let $\hat{\boldsymbol{\eta}}_{\mathcal{F}} := ([\mathcal{F}] - \top) / \|[\mathcal{F}] - \top\|_2$, then it is easy to show that the gradients with respect to relation embedding $[R]$ and entity pair embedding $[p]$ are

$$\partial/\partial\,[p] = [R]\,\hat{\boldsymbol{\eta}}_{\mathcal{F}} \quad \text{and} \quad \partial/\partial\,[R] = \hat{\boldsymbol{\eta}}_{\mathcal{F}} \otimes [p] .$$

3.3 First-order Formulae

Crucially, and in contrast to matrix factorization, we can inject more expressive logical formulae than just ground atoms. For example, the KB K may contain a universally quantified first-order rule such as $\forall x : R_1(x) \implies R_2(x)$. Assuming a finite domain, this statement can be unrolled into a conjunction of propositional statements of the form $\mathcal{F} = R_1(p) \implies R_2(p)$, one for each pair p. We can directly inject these propositional statements into the embeddings, and their gradients are straightfoward to derive. For example,

$$\partial/\partial\,[R_1] = (([\implies] \times_2 [R_2(p)])\,\hat{\boldsymbol{\eta}}_{\mathcal{F}}) \otimes [p] .$$

3.4 Learning and Inference

We learn embeddings for entity pairs and relations by minimizing objective 1 using stochastic gradient descent (SGD). To infer the (two-dimensional) truth value (C in Figure 1) of a formula $\mathcal{F}$ in embedded logic we evaluate $[\mathcal{F}]$. An easier to intpret one-dimensional representation can be derived by

$$\left(\langle[\mathcal{F}], \begin{bmatrix}1 & -1\end{bmatrix}^T\rangle + 1\right)/2,$$

followed by truncation to the interval $[0, 1]$. Other ways of projecting $[\mathcal{F}]$ to $\mathbb{R}$, such as using cosine similarity to $\top$, are possible as well.

4 Experiments

We perform experiments on synthetic data defined over 7 entity pairs and 6 relations. We fix the embedding size k to 4 and train the model for 100 epochs using SGD with ℓ_2-regularization on the values of the embeddings. The learning rate and the regularization parameter are set to 0.05.

The left part of Table 1 shows the observed (bold) and inferred truth values for a set of factual staments of the form $R(p)$, mapped to $\mathbb{R}$ as discussed above. Due to the generalization obtained by low-dimensional embeddings, the model infers that, for example, SMITH is an employee at CAMBRIDGE and DAVIES lives in LONDON. However, we would like the model to also capture that every professor works for his or her university

	With Factual Constraints						With Factual and First-Order Constraints					
	profAt	*worksFor*	*employeeAt*	*registeredIn*	*livesIn*	*bornIn*	*profAt*	*worksFor*	*employeeAt*	*registeredIn*	*livesIn*	*bornIn*
⟨JONES, UWASH⟩	**1.00**	**1.00**	**1.00**	0.00	0.18	0.01	**0.98**	**0.98**	**0.95**	0.03	0.00	0.04
⟨TAYLOR, UCL⟩	**1.00**	**1.00**	**0.98**	0.00	0.20	0.00	**0.98**	**0.96**	**0.95**	0.05	0.00	0.06
⟨SMITH, CAMBRIDGE⟩	**0.98**	$^\top$ 0.00	$^\top$ 0.64	0.75	0.07	0.72	**0.92**	$^\top$ 0.97	$^\top$ 0.89	0.04	0.04	0.05
⟨WILLIAMS, OXFORD⟩	$^\perp$ 0.02	**1.00**	0.08	0.00	0.93	0.02	$^\perp$ 0.05	**0.91**	0.02	0.05	0.87	0.06
⟨BROWN, CAMBRIDGE⟩	$^\perp$ 0.00	**0.97**	0.02	$^\perp$ 0.01	**0.95**	0.06	$^\perp$ 0.01	**0.90**	0.00	$^\perp$ 0.07	**0.92**	0.07
⟨DAVIES, LONDON⟩	0.00	0.00	0.00	**0.99**	$^\top$ 0.50	**1.00**	0.01	0.00	0.00	**0.98**	$^\top$ 0.98	**0.97**
⟨EVANS, PARIS⟩	0.00	0.00	0.00	**1.00**	$^\top$ 0.48	**1.00**	0.00	0.00	0.00	**0.97**	$^\top$ 1.00	**0.96**

Table 1: Reconstructed matrix without (left) and with (right) the first-order constraints $profAt \implies worksFor$ and $registeredIn \implies livesIn$. Predictions for training cells of factual constraints $[R(p)] = \top$ are shown in bold, and `true` and `false` test cells are denoted by $^\top$ and $^\perp$ respectively.

and that, when somebody is registered in a city, he or she also lives in that city.

When including such first-order constraints (right part of Table 1), the model's predictions improve concerning different aspects. First, the model gets the implication right, demonstrating that the low-dimensional embeddings encode first-order knowledge. Second, this implication transitively improves the predictions on other columns (*e.g.* SMITH is an employee at CAMBRIDGE). Third, the implication works indeed in an asymmetric way, *e.g.*, the model does not predict that WILLIAMS is a professor at OXFORD just because she is working there.

5 Related Work

The idea of bringing together distributional semantics and formal logic is not new. Lewis and Steedman (2013) improve the generalization performance of a semantic parser via the use of distributional representations. However, their target representation language is still symbolic, and it is unclear how this approach can cope with noise and uncertainty in data.

Another line of work (Clark and Pulman, 2007; Mitchell and Lapata, 2008; Coecke et al., 2010; Socher et al., 2012; Hermann and Blunsom, 2013) uses symbolic representations to guide the composition of distributional representations. Reading a sentence or logical formula there amounts to compositionally mapping it to a k-dimensional vector that then can be used for downstream tasks. We propose a very different approach: Reading a sentence amounts to updating the involved entity pair and relation embeddings such that the sentence evaluates to *true*. Afterwards we cannot use the embeddings to calculate sentence similarities, but to answer relational questions about the world.

Similar to our work, Bowman (2014) provides further evidence that distributed representations can indeed capture logical reasoning. Although Bowman demonstrates this on natural logic expressions without capturing factual statements, one can think of ways to include the latter in his framework as well. However, the approach presented here can conceptually inject complex nested logical statements into embeddings, whereas it is not obvious how this can be achieved in the neural-network based multi-class classification framework proposed by Bowman.

6 Conclusion

We have argued that low dimensional embeddings of entities and relations may be tuned to simulate the behavior of logic and hence combine the advantages of distributional representations with those of their symbolic counterparts. As a first step into this direction we have presented an objective that encourages embeddings to be consistent with a given logical knowledge base that includes facts and first-order rules. On a small synthetic dataset we optimize this objective with SGD to learn low-dimensional embeddings that indeed follow the behavior of the knowledge base.

Clearly we have only scratched the surface here. Besides only using toy data and logical formulae of very limited expressiveness, there are fundamental questions we have yet to address. For example, even if the embeddings could enable perfect logical reasoning, how do we provide provenance or proofs of answers? Moreover, in practice a machine reader (*e.g.* a semantic parser) *incrementally* gathers logical statements from text— how could we *incrementally* inject this knowledge into embeddings without retraining the whole model? Finally, what are the theoretical limits of embedding logic in vector spaces?

Acknowledgments

We would like to thank Giorgos Spithourakis, Thore Graepel, Karl Moritz Hermann and Edward Grefenstette for helpful discussions, and Andreas Vlachos for comments on the manuscript. This work was supported by Microsoft Research through its PhD Scholarship Programme. This work was supported in part by the TerraSwarm Research Center, one of six centers supported by the STARnet phase of the Focus Center Research Program (FCRP) a Semiconductor Research Corporation program sponsored by MARCO and DARPA.

References

Antoine Bordes, Jason Weston, Ronan Collobert, and Yoshua Bengio. 2011. Learning structured embeddings of knowledge bases. In *AAAI*.

Johan Bos and Katja Markert. 2005. Recognising textual entailment with logical inference. In *Proc. of HLT/EMNLP*, pages 628–635.

Samuel R Bowman. 2014. Can recursive neural tensor networks learn logical reasoning? In *ICLR'14*.

Stephen Clark and Stephen Pulman. 2007. Combining symbolic and distributional models of meaning. In *AAAI Spring Symposium: Quantum Interaction*, pages 52–55.

Bob Coecke, Mehrnoosh Sadrzadeh, and Stephen Clark. 2010. Mathematical foundations for a compositional distributional model of meaning. *CoRR*, abs/1003.4394.

Edward Grefenstette. 2013. Towards a formal distributional semantics: Simulating logical calculi with tensors. In *Proc. of *SEM*, pages 1–10.

Karl Moritz Hermann and Phil Blunsom. 2013. The role of syntax in vector space models of compositional semantics. In *Proc. of ACL*, pages 894–904.

Tamara G Kolda and Brett W Bader. 2009. Tensor decompositions and applications. *SIAM review*, 51(3):455–500.

Mike Lewis and Mark Steedman. 2013. Combined distributional and logical semantics. In *TACL*, volume 1, pages 179–192.

Mike Mintz, Steven Bills, Rion Snow, and Daniel Jurafsky. 2009. Distant supervision for relation extraction without labeled data. In *Proc. of ACL-IJCNLP*, pages 1003–1011.

Jeff Mitchell and Mirella Lapata. 2008. Vector-based models of semantic composition. In *Proc. of ACL*, pages 236–244.

Sebastian Riedel, Limin Yao, Andrew McCallum, and Benjamin M Marlin. 2013. Relation extraction with matrix factorization and universal schemas. In *Proc. of NAACL-HLT*, pages 74–84.

Richard Socher, Brody Huval, Christopher D Manning, and Andrew Y Ng. 2012. Semantic compositionality through recursive matrix-vector spaces. In *Proc. of EMNLP*, pages 1201–1211.

Luke S Zettlemoyer and Michael Collins. 2005. Learning to map sentences to logical form: Structured classification with probabilistic categorial grammars. In *Proc. of UAI*, pages 658–666.

Software Requirements: A new Domain for Semantic Parsers

Michael Roth† Themistoklis Diamantopoulos‡ Ewan Klein† Andreas Symeonidis‡
†ILCC, School of Informatics
University of Edinburgh
{mroth,ewan}@inf.ed.ac.uk
‡Electrical & Computer Engineering Department
Aristotle University of Thessaloniki
thdiaman@issel.ee.auth.gr
asymeon@eng.auth.gr

Abstract

Software requirements are commonly written in natural language, making them prone to ambiguity, incompleteness and inconsistency. By converting requirements to formal semantic representations, emerging problems can be detected at an early stage of the development process, thus reducing the number of ensuing errors and the development costs. In this paper, we treat the mapping from requirements to formal representations as a semantic parsing task. We describe a novel data set for this task that involves two contributions: first, we establish an ontology for formally representing requirements; and second, we introduce an iterative annotation scheme, in which formal representations are derived through step-wise refinements.

1 Introduction

During the process of software development, developers and customers typically discuss and agree on requirements that specify the functionality of a system that is being developed.[1] Such requirements play a crucial role in the development lifecycle, as they form the basis for actual implementations, corresponding work plans, cost estimations and follow-up directives (van Lamsweerde, 2009). In general, software requirements can be expressed in various different ways, including the use of UML diagrams and storyboards. Most commonly, however, expectations are expressed in natural language (Mich et al., 2004), as shown in Example (1):

(1) A user should be able to login to his account.

[1]Although software engineering can also involve *non-functional* requirements, which describe general quality criteria of a system, this paper is only concerned with functional requirements, i.e., requirements that specify the behavior of a system.

While requirements expressed in natural language have the advantage of being intelligible to both clients and developers, they can of course also be ambiguous, vague and incomplete. Although formal languages could be used as an alternative that eliminates some of these problems, customers are rarely equipped with the mathematical and technical expertise for understanding highly formalised requirements. To benefit from the advantages of both natural language and formal representations, we propose to induce the latter automatically from text in a semantic parsing task. Given the software requirement in Example (1), for instance, we would like to construct a representation that explicitly specifies the types of the entities involved (e.g., *object*(account)) and that captures explicit and inferable relationships among them (e.g., *owns*(user, account)). We expect such formal representations to be helpful in detecting errors at an early stage of the development process (e.g., via logical inference and verification tools), thus avoiding the costs of finding and fixing problems at a later and hence more expensive stage (Boehm and Basili, 2001).

Given the benefits of formal representations, we believe that software requirements constitute a useful application domain for semantic parsers. Requirement texts naturally occur in the real world and appropriate data sets can thus be constructed without setting up artificial tasks to collect them. Parsing requirements of different software projects also poses interesting challenges as texts exhibit a considerable amount of lexical variety, while frequently also containing more than one relation per sentence.

2 Related Work

A range of methods have been proposed in previous work to (semi-)automatically process requirements written in plain, natural language text and map them to formal representations. To the best

Proceedings of the ACL 2014 Workshop on Semantic Parsing, pages 50–54,
Baltimore, Maryland USA, June 26 2014.

of our knowledge, Abbott (1983) was the first to introduce a technique for extracting data types, variables and operators from informal texts describing a problem. The proposed method follows a simple rule-based setup, in which common nouns are identified as data types, proper nouns as objects and verbs as operators between them. Booch (1986) described a method of similar complexity that extends Abbot's approach to object-oriented development. Saeki et al. (1989) implemented a first prototype that automatically constructs object-oriented models from informal requirements. As proposed by Abbott and Booch, the system is based on automatically extracted nouns and verbs. Although Saeki et al. found resulting object diagrams of reasonable quality, they concluded that human intervention was still necessary to distinguish between words that are relevant for the model and irrelevant nouns and verbs. Nanduri and Rugaber (1995) proposed to further automate object-oriented analysis of requirement texts by applying a syntactic parser and a set of post-processing rules. In a similar setting, Mich (1996) employed a full NLP pipeline that contains a semantic analysis module, thus omitting the need for additional post-processing rules. More recent approaches include those by Harmain and Gaizauskas (2003) and Kof (2004), who relied on a combination of NLP components and human interaction. Whereas most approaches in previous work aim to derive class diagrams, Ghosh et al. (2014) proposed a pipeline architecture that converts syntactic parses to logical expressions via a set of heuristic post-processing rules.

Despite this seemingly long tradition, previous methods for processing software requirements have tended to depend on domain-specific heuristics and knowledge bases or have required additional user intervention. In contrast, we propose to utilize annotated data to learn how to perform semantic parsing of requirements automatically.

3 Data Set

Given our conviction that mapping natural language software requirements to formal representations provides an attractive challenge for semantic parsing research, we believe that there is a more general benefit in building a corpus of annotated requirements. One immediate obstacle is that software requirements can drastically differ in quality, style and granularity. To cover a range of possible differences, we asked lecturers from several universities to provide requirement documents written by students. We received requirement documents on student projects from various domains, including embedded systems, virtual reality and web applications.[2] From these documents, we extracted lists of requirements, each of which is expressed within a single sentence. We additionally collected single sentence requirements within the S-CASE project, describing industrial prototypes of cloud-based web services.[3] Table 1 gives an overview of the quantity of requirements collected. We observe that the number of requirements received for student projects is much higher. The token counts reveal however that requirements written for industrial prototypes are longer on average (16.6 vs. 11.6 words). This observation might be related to the fact that students in software engineering classes are often provided with explicit guidelines on how to concisely express requirements in natural language. As a consequence, we also find their requirement texts to be more regimented and stylised than those written by senior software engineers. Examples (2) and (3) show examples of a student-written and developer-written requirement, respectively.

	#sentences	#tokens	#types
student projects	270	3130	604
industrial prototypes	55	927	286
Our dataset (total)	325	4057	765
GEOQUERY880	880	6656	279
FREE917	917	6769	2035

Table 1: Statistics on our requirements collection and existing semantic parsing data sets.

(2) The user must be able to vote on polls.

(3) For each user contact, back-end must perform a check to determine whether the contact is a registered user or not.

In comparison to two extant data sets, namely GeoQuery880 (Tang, 2003) and Free917 (Cai and Yates, 2013), we find that our collection is still relatively small in terms of example sentences. The

[2]The majority of collected requirements are from a software development course organized jointly by several European universities, cf. `http://www.fer.unizg.hr/rasip/dsd`

[3]`http://www.scasefp7.eu/`

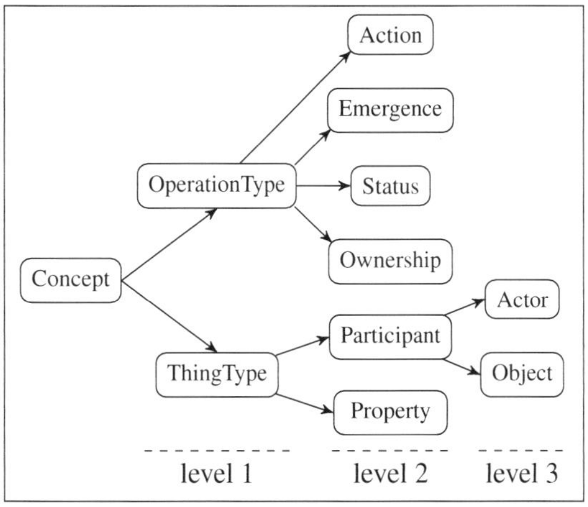

Figure 1: Class hierarchy of our conceptual ontology for modeling software requirements.

difference in total number of tokens is not as crucial, however, given that sentences in our data set are much longer on average. We further observe that the token/type ratio in our texts lies somewhere between ratios reported in previous work. Based on the observed lexical variety and average sentence length, we expect our texts to be challenging but not too difficult to parse using existing methods.

4 Modeling Requirements Conceptually

Different representations have been proposed for modeling requirements in previous work: whereas early work focused on deriving simple class diagrams, more recent approaches suggest representing requirements via logical forms (cf. Section 2).

In this paper, we propose to model requirements using a formal ontology that captures general concepts from different application domains. Our proposed ontology covers the same properties as earlier work and provides a means to represent requirements in logical form. In practice, such logical forms can be induced by semantic parsers and in subsequent steps be utilized for automatic inference. The class hierarchy of our ontology is shown in Figure 1. At the highest level of the class hierarchy, we distinguish between "things" (*ThingType*) and "operations" (*OperationType*).

4.1 ThingType

We define the following subclasses of *ThingType*:

- A *Participant* is a thing that is involved in an operation. We further subdivide *Participants* into *Actors*, which can be users of a system or the system itself, and *Objects*.
- A *Property* is an attribute of an *Object* or a characteristic of an *OperationType*.

4.2 OperationType

We further divide operations into the following subclasses:

- An *Action* describes an operation that is performed by an *Actor* on one or several *Object*(s).
- A *State* is an operation that describes the status of an *Actor*.
- *Ownership* is used to model operations that express possession.
- *Emergence* represent operations that undergo passive transformation.

4.3 Relations

In addition to the class hierarchy, we define a set of relations between classes, which describe and constrain how different operations and things can interact with each other.

On the level of *OperationType*, every operation can be assigned one *Actor* via the relations HAS_ACTOR or HAS_OWNER, respectively. *Objects* can participate in *Actions*, *States* and *Ownerships* via the relations ACTS_ON, HAS_STATE and OWNS, respectively. Every instance of *OperationType* and *Object* can further have an arbitrary number of properties assigned to it via the relation HAS_PROPERTY.

5 Annotation Process

In preliminary annotation experiments, we found that class diagrams may be too simple to represent requirements conceptually. Logical forms, on the other hand, can be difficult to use for annotators without sufficient background knowledge. To keep the same level of expressiveness as logical forms and the simplicity of object-oriented annotations, we propose a multi-step annotation scheme, in which decisions in one iteration are further refined in later iterations.

By adopting the class hierarchy introduced in Section 4, we can naturally divide each annotation iteration according to a level in the ontology. This means that in the first iteration, we ask annotators

A user that is logged in to his account must be able to update his password.		
Actor(user)	$\wedge$ *Action*(login)	$\wedge$ *Action*(update)
$\wedge$ *Object*(account)	$\wedge$ HAS_ACTOR(login,user)	$\wedge$ HAS_ACTOR(update,user)
$\wedge$ *Object*(password)	$\wedge$ ACTS_ON(login,account)	$\wedge$ ACTS_ON(update,password)
	$\wedge$ *Ownership*(o_1)	$\wedge$ *Ownership*(o_2)
	$\wedge$ HAS_OWNER(o_1,user)	$\wedge$ HAS_OWNER(o_2,user)
	$\wedge$ OWNS(o_1,account)	$\wedge$ OWNS(o_2,password)
The system must be able to forward and rewind a playing program.		
Actor(system)	$\wedge$ *Action*(forward)	$\wedge$ *Action*(rewind)
$\wedge$ *Object*(program)	$\wedge$ HAS_ACTOR(forward,system)	$\wedge$ HAS_ACTOR(rewind,system)
	$\wedge$ ACTS_ON(forward,program)	$\wedge$ ACTS_ON(rewind,program)
	$\wedge$ *Property*(playing)	$\wedge$ HAS_PROPERTY(program,playing)

Table 2: Example requirements from different domains and logical forms derived from annotations.

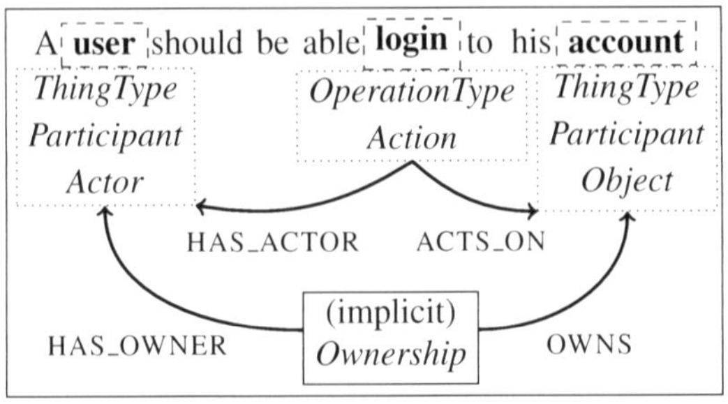

Figure 2: Annotation process: instances are marked in text (dashed), class assignments are refined (dotted), and relations are added (solid).

to simply mark all instances of *ThingType* and *OperationType* that are explicitly expressed in a given requirement. We then resolve conflicting annotations and present the resulting instances from the first level to annotators for the next iteration. In each iteration, we add one layer of sophistication from the class hierarchy, resulting in step-wise refinements. In the final iteration, we add relations between instances of concepts, including implicit but inferable cases.

An illustration of the overall annotation process, based on Example (1), is depicted in Figure 2. The last iteration in this example involves the addition of an *Ownership* instance that is indicated (by the phrase "his account") but not explicitly realized in text. Although identifying and annotating such instances can be more challenging than the previous annotation steps, we can directly populate our ontology at this stage (e.g., via conversion to RDF tuples) and run verification tools to check whether they are consistent with the annotation schema.

6 Discussion

The annotation scheme introduced in Section 4 is designed with the goal of covering a wide range of different application domains. Although this means that many of the more fine-grained distinctions within a domain are not considered here, we believe that the scheme already provides sufficient information for a range of tasks. By storing processed requirements in a relational database, for example, they can be retrieved using structured queries and utilized for probabilistic inference.

Given the hierarchical structure of our annotation process, as defined in Section 5, it is possible to extend existing annotations with additional levels of granularity provided by domain ontologies. As an example, we have defined a domain ontology for web services, which contains subclasses of *Action* to further distinguish between the HTTP methods *get*, *put*, *post* and *delete*. Similar extensions can be defined for other domains.

Regarding the task of semantic parsing itself, we are currently in the process of annotating several hundreds of instances of requirements (cf. Section 3) following the proposed ontology. We will release an initial version of this data set at the Semantic Parsing workshop. The initial release will serve as a basis for training and evaluating parsers in this domain, for which we are also planning to collect more examples throughout the year. We believe that requirements form an interesting domain for the parsing community as the texts involve a fair amount of variation and challenging semantic phenomena (such as inferable relations), while also serving a practical and valuable purpose.

Acknowledgements

Parts of this work have been supported by the FP7 Collaborative Project S-CASE (Grant Agreement No 610717), funded by the European Commission. We thank our project partners for data support and useful discussions on the proposed ontology.

References

Russell J Abbott. 1983. Program design by informal english descriptions. *Communications of the ACM*, 26(11):882–894.

Barry Boehm and Victor R. Basili. 2001. Software defect reduction top 10 list. *Computer*, 34:135–137.

Grady Booch. 1986. Object-oriented development. *IEEE Transactions on Software Engineering*, (2):211–221.

Qingqing Cai and Alexander Yates. 2013. Large-scale semantic parsing via schema matching and lexicon extension. In *Proceedings of the 51st Annual Meeting of the Association for Computational Linguistics (Volume 1: Long Papers)*, pages 423–433, Sofia, Bulgaria, August.

Shalini Ghosh, Daniel Elenius, Wenchao Li, Patrick Lincoln, Natarajan Shankar, and Wilfried Steiner. 2014. Automatically extracting requirements specifications from natural language. *arXiv preprint arXiv:1403.3142*.

H. M. Harmain and Robert Gaizauskas. 2003. Cm-builder: A natural language-based case tool for object-oriented analysis. *Automated Software Engineering*, 10(2):157–181.

Leonid Kof. 2004. Natural language processing for requirements engineering: Applicability to large requirements documents. In *19th International Conference on Automated Software Engineering, Workshop Proceedings*.

Luisa Mich, Franch Mariangela, and Novi Inverardi Pierluigi. 2004. Market research for requirements analysis using linguistic tools. *Requirements Engineering*, 9(1):40–56.

Luisa Mich. 1996. NL-OOPS: From natural language to object oriented requirements using the natural language processing system LOLITA. *Natural Language Engineering*, 2(2):161–187.

Sastry Nanduri and Spencer Rugaber. 1995. Requirements validation via automated natural language parsing. In *Proceedings of the Twenty-Eighth Hawaii International Conference on System Sciences*, volume 3, pages 362–368.

Motoshi Saeki, Hisayuki Horai, and Hajime Enomoto. 1989. Software development process from natural language specification. In *Proceedings of the 11th International Conference on Software Engineering*, pages 64–73.

Lappoon R. Tang. 2003. *Integrating Top-down and Bottom-up Approaches in Inductive Logic Programming: Applications in Natural Language Processing and Relational Data Mining*. Ph.D. thesis, Department of Computer Sciences, University of Texas, Austin, Texas, USA, August.

Axel van Lamsweerde. 2009. *Requirements Engineering: From System Goals to UML Models to Software Specifications*. Wiley.

From Treebank Parses to Episodic Logic and Commonsense Inference

Lenhart Schubert
Univ. of Rochester
schubert@cs.rochester.edu

1. Introduction and overview

We have developed an approach to broad-coverage semantic parsing that starts with Treebank parses and yields scoped, deindexed formulas in Episodic Logic (EL) that are directly usable for knowledge-based inference. Distinctive properties of our approach are

- the use of a tree transduction language, TTT, to partially disambiguate, refine (and sometimes repair) raw Treebank parses, and also to perform many deindexing and logical canonicalization tasks;
- the use of EL, a Montague-inspired logical framework for semantic representation and knowledge representation;
- allowance for nonclassical restricted quantifiers, several forms of modification and reification, quasi-quotes and syntactic closures;
- an event semantics that directly represents events with complex characterizations;
- a scoping algorithm that heuristically scopes quantifiers, logical connectives, and tense;
- a compositional approach to tense deindexing making use of tense trees; and
- the use of an inference engine, EPILOG, that supports input-driven and goal-driven inference in EL, in a style similar to (but more general than) Natural Logic.

We have applied this framework to general knowledge acquisition from text corpora and the web (though with tense meaning and many other semantic details stripped away) (e.g., Schubert & Hwang 2000, Van Durme & Schubert 2008), and more recently to caption interpretation for family photos, enabling alignment of names and other descriptors with human faces in the photos, and to interpreting sentences in simple first-reader stories. Ongoing projects are aimed at full interpretation of lexical glosses and other sources of explicitly expressed general knowledge.

We now elaborate some of the themes in the preceding overview, concluding with comments on related work and important remaining challenges.

2. Refinement of Treebank parses using TTT

We generate initial logical forms by compositional interpretation of Treebank parses produced by the Charniak parser.[1] This mapping is encumbered by a number of difficulties. One is that current Treebank parsers produce many thousands of distinct expansions of phrasal categories, especially VPs, into sequences of constituents. We have overcome this difficulty through use of enhanced regular-expression patterns applied to sequences of constituent types, where our interpretive rules are associated directly with these patterns. About 100 patterns and corresponding semantic rules cover most of English.

Two other difficulties are that parsers still introduce about one phrasal error for every 10 words, and these can render interpretations nonsensical; and even when parses are deemed correct according to "gold standard" annotated corpora, they often conflate semantically disparate word and phrase types. For example, prepositional phrases (PPs) functioning as predicates are not distinguished from ones functioning as adverbial modifiers; the roles of wh-words that form questions, relative clauses, or wh-nominals are not distinguished; and constituents parsed as SBARs (subordinate clauses) can be relative clauses, adverbials, question clauses, or clausal nominals. Our approach to these problems makes use of a new tree transduction language, TTT (Purtee & Schubert 2012) that allows concise, modular, declarative representation of tree transductions. (As indicated below, TTT also plays a key role in logical form postprocessing.) While we cannot ex-

[1] ftp://ftp.cs.brown.edu/pub/nlparser/

Proceedings of the ACL 2014 Workshop on Semantic Parsing, pages 55–60,
Baltimore, Maryland USA, June 26 2014.

pect to correct the majority of parse errors in general texts, we have found it easy to use TTT for correction of certain systematic errors in particular domains. In addition, we use TTT to subclassify many function words and phrase types, and to partially disambiguate the role of PPs and SBARs, among other phrase types, allowing more reliable semantic interpretation.

3. EL as a semantic representation and knowledge representation

From a compositional perspective, the semantics of natural language is intensional and richly expressive, allowing for nonclassical quantifiers and several types of modification and reification. Yet many approaches to semantic interpretation rely on first-order logic (FOL) or some subset thereof as their target semantic representation. This is justifiable in certain restricted applications, grounded in extensional domains such as databases. However, FOL or description logics are often chosen as the semantic target even for broad-coverage semantic parsing, because of their well-understood semantics and proof theory and well-developed inference technology and, in some cases, by a putative expressiveness-tractability tradeoff. We reject such motivations – tools should be made to fit the phenomenon rather than the other way around. The tractability argument, for example, is simply mistaken: Efficient inference algorithms for subsets of an expressive representation can also be implemented within a more comprehensive inference framework, without forfeiting the advantages of expressiveness. Moreover, recent work in Natural Logic, which uses phrase-structured NL directly for inference, indicates that the richness of language is no obstacle to rapid inference of many obvious lexical entailments (e.g., MacCartney & Manning 2009).

Thus our target representation, EL, taking its cue from Montague allows directly for the kinds of quantification, intensionality, modification, and reification found in all natural languages (e.g., Schubert & Hwang 2000, Schubert, to appear). In addition, EL associates episodes (events, situations, processes) directly with arbitrarily complex sentences, rather than just with atomic predications, as in Davidsonian event semantics. For example, the initial sentence in each of the following pairs is interpreted as directly characterizing an episode, which then serves as antecedent for a pronoun or definite:

For many months, no rain fell;
this totally dried out the topsoil.

Each superpower menaced the other with its nuclear arsenal; this situation persisted for decades.

Also, since NL allows for discussion of linguistic and other symbolic entities, so does EL, via quasi-quotation and substitutional quantification (closures). These can also express axiom schemas, and autocognitive reasoning (see further comments in Section 5).

4. Comprehensive scoping and tense deindexing

Though EL is Montague-inspired, one difference from a Montague-style intensional logic is that we treat noun phrase (NP) interpretations as unscoped elements, rather than second-order predicates. These elements are heuristically scoped to the sentence level in LF postprocessing, as proposed in (Schubert & Pelletier 1982). The latter proposal also covered scoping of logical connectives, which exhibit the same scope ambiguities as quantifiers. Our current heuristic scoping algorithm handles these phenomena as well as tense scope, allowing for such factors as syntactic ordering, island constraints, and differences in wide-scoping tendencies among different operators.

Episodes characterized by sentences remain implicit until application of a "deindexing" algorithm. This algorithm makes use of a contextual element called a *tense tree* which is built and traversed in accordance with simple recursive rules applied to indexical LFs. A tense tree contains branches corresponding to tense and aspect operators, and in the course of processing one or more sentences, sequences of episode tokens corresponding to clauses are deposited at the nodes by the deindexing rules, and adjacent tokens are used by these same rules to posit temporal or causal relations among "evoked" episodes. A comprehensive set of rules covering all tenses, aspects, and temporal adverbials was specified in (Hwang & Schubert 1994); the current semantic parsing machinery incorporates the tense and aspect rules but not yet the temporal adverbial rules.

Further processing steps, many implemented through TTT rules, further transform the LFs so as to Skolemize top-level existentials and definite NPs (in effect accommodating their presuppositions), separate top-level conjuncts, narrow the scopes of certain negations, widen quantifier scopes out of episodic operator scopes where possible, resolve intrasentential coreference, perform lambda and equality reductions, and also generate some immediate inferences (e.g., inferring that *Mrs. Smith* refers to a married woman).

The following example, for the first sentence above, illustrates the kind of LF generated by our semantic parser (first in unscoped, indexical form, then the resulting set of scoped, deindexed, and canonicalized formulas). Note that EL uses predicate infixing at the sentence level, for readability; so for example we have (E0 BEFORE NOW0) rather than (BEFORE E0 NOW0). '**' is the operator linking a sentential formula to the episode it characterizes (Schubert 2000). ADV-S is a type-shifting operator, L stands for λ, and PLUR is a predicate modifer that converts a predicate over individuals into a predicate over sets of individuals.

For many months, no rain fell;

Refined Treebank parse:

(S (PP-FOR (IN for) (NP (CD many) (NNS months))) (|,| |,|)
(NP (DT no) (NN rain)) (VP (VBD fell)) (|:| |;|))

Unscoped, indexical LF (keys :F, :P, etc., are dropped later):

(:F (:F ADV-S (:P FOR.P (:Q MANY.DET (:F PLUR MONTH.N))))
(:I (:Q NO.DET RAIN.N) (:O PAST FALL.V)))

Canonicalized LFs (without adverbial-modifier deindexing):

(MONTHS0.SK (PLUR MONTH.N)), (MONTHS0.SK MANY.A),
((ADV-S (L Y (Y FOR.P MONTHS0.SK)))
((NO Z (Z RAIN.N) (SOME E0 (E0 BEFORE NOW0)
(Z FALL.V))) ** E0)

With adverbial deindexing, the prefixed adverbial modifier would become a predication (**E0 LASTS-FOR.V MONTHS0.SK**); **E0** is the episode of no rain falling and **MONTHS0.SK** is the Skolem name generated for the set of many months.

5. Inference using the EPILOG inference engine

Semantic parsers that employ FOL or a subset of FOL (such as a description logic) as the target representation often employ an initial "abstract" representation mirroring some of the expressive devices of natural languages, which is then mapped to the target representation enabling inference. An important feature of our approach is that (scoped, deindexed) LFs expressed in EL are directly usable for inference in conjunction with lexical and world knowledge by our EPILOG inference engine. This has the advantages of not sacrificing any of the expressiveness of language, of linking inference more directly to surface form (in principle enabling incremental entailment inference), and of being easier to understand and edit than representations remote from language.

EPILOG's two main inference rules, for input-driven (forward-chaining) and goal-driven (backward-chaining) inference, substitute consequences or anti-consequences for subformulas as a function of polarity, much as in Natural Logic. But substitutions can be based on world knowledge as well as lexical knowledge, and to assure first-order completeness the chaining rules are supplemented with natural deduction rules such as proof by contradiction and proof of conditional formulas by assumption of the antecedent.

Moreover, EPILOG can reason with the expressive devices of EL mentioned in Sections 1 and 3 that lie beyond FOL, including generalized quantifiers, and reified predicates and propositions. (Schubert, to appear) contains relevant examples, such as the inference from *Most of the heavy Monroe resources are located in Monroe-east*, and background knowledge, to the conclusion *Few heavy resources are located in Monroe-west*; and inference of an answer to the modally complex question *Can the small crane be used to hoist rubble from the collapsed building on Penfield Rd onto a truck?* Also, the ability to use axiom schemas that involve quasi-quotes and syntactic closures allows lexical inferences based on knowledge about syntactic classes of lexical items (i.e., meaning postulates), as well as various forms of metareasoning, including reasoning about the system's own knowledge and perceptions (Morbini & Schubert 2011). Significantly, the expressiveness of EL/EPILOG does not prevent competitive performance on first-order commonsense knowledge bases (derived from Doug Lenat's Cyc), especially as the number of KB formulas grows into the thousands (Morbini & Schubert 2009).

In the various inference tasks to which EPILOG was applied in the past, the LFs used for natural language sentences were based on presumed compositional rules, without the machinery to derive them automatically (e.g., Schubert & Hwang 2000, Morbini & Schubert 2011, Stratos et al. 2011). Starting in 2001, in developing our KNEXT system for knowledge extraction from text, we used broad-coverage compositional interpretion into EL for the first time, but since our goal was to obtain simple general "factoids"–such as that *a person may believe a proposition, people may wish to get rid of a dictator, clothes can be washed, etc.* (expressed logically)–our interpretive rules ignored tense, many modifiers, and other subtleties (e.g., Van Durme & Schubert 2008).

Factoids like the ones mentioned are unconditional and as such not directly usable for inference, but many millions of the factoids have been automatically strengthened into quantified, inference-enabling commonsense axioms (Gordon & Schubert 2010), and allow EPILOG to draw conclusions from short sentences (Gordon 2014, chapter 6). An example is the inference from *Tremblay is a singer* to the conclusion *Quite possibly Tremblay occasionally performs (or performed) a song* (automatically verbalized from an EL formula). Here the modal and frequency modification would not easily be captured within an FOL framework.

Recently, we have begun to apply much more complete compositional semantic rules to sentences "in the wild", choosing two settings where sentences tend to be short (to minimize the impact of parse errors on semantic interpretation): derivation and integration of caption-derived knowledge and image-derived knowledge in a family photo domain, and interpretation of sentences in first-reader stories. In the family photo domain, we have fully interpreted the captions in a small development set, and used an EPILOG knowledge base to derive implicit attributes of the individuals mentioned in the captions (by name or other designations). These attributes then served to align the caption-derived individuals with individuals detected in the images, and were subsequently merged with image-derived attributes (with allowance for uncertainty). For example, for the caption *Tanya and Grandma Lillian at her high school graduation party*, after correct interpretation of *her* as referring to Tanya, Tanya was inferred to be a teenager (from the knowledge that a high school graduation party is generally held for a recent high school graduate, and a recent high school graduate is likely to be a teenager); while Grandma Lillian was inferred to be a grandmother, hence probably a senior, hence quite possibly gray-haired, and this enabled correct alignment of the names with the persons detected in the image, determined via image processing to be a young dark-haired female and a senior gray-haired female respectively.

In the first-reader domain (where we are using McGuffey (2005)), we found that we could obtain correct or nearly correct interpretations for most simple declaratives (and some of the stories consist entirely of such sentences). At the time of writing, we are still working on discourse phenomena, especially in stories involving dialogues. For example, our semantic parser correctly derived and canonicalized the logical content of the opening line of one of the stories under consideration,

Oh Rosie! Do you see that nest in the apple tree?

The interpretation includes separate speech acts for the initial interjection and the question. Our goal in this work is integration of symbolic inference with inferences from imagistic modeling (for which we are using the Blender open source software), where the latter provides spatial inferences such as that the contents of a nest in a tree are not likely to be visible to children on the ground (setting the stage for the continuation of the story).

Phenomena not handled well at this point include intersentential anaphora, questions with gaps, imperatives, interjections, and direct address (*Look, Lucy, ...*). We are making progress on these, by using TTT repair rules for phenomena where Treebank parsers tend to falter, and by adding LF-level and discourse-level interpretive rules for the resulting phrasal patterns. Ongoing projects are aimed at full interpretation of lexical glosses and other sources of explicitly expressed general knowledge. However, as we explain in the concluding section, we do not believe that full-fledged, deep story understanding will be possible until we have large amounts of general knowledge, including not only the kinds of "if-then" knowledge (about word meanings and the world) we and others have been deriving and are continuing to derive, but also large amounts of pattern-like, schematic knowledge encoding our expectations about typical object configurations and event sequences (especially ones directed towards agents' goals) in the world and in dialogue.

6. Related work

Most current projects in semantic parsing either single out domains that assure highly restricted natural language usage, or greatly limit the semantic content that is extracted from text. For example, projects may be aimed at question-answering over relational databases, with themes such as geography, air travel planning, or robocup (e.g., Ge & Mooney 2009, Artzi & Zettlemoyer 2011,

Kwiatkowski et al. 2011, Liang et al. 2011, Poon 2013). Impressive thematic scope is achieved in (Berant et al. 2013, Kwiatkowski et al. 2013), but the target semantic language (for Freebase access) is still restricted to database operations such as join, intersection, and set cardinality. Another popular domain is command execution by robots (e.g., Tellex 2011, Howard et al. 2013, Artzi & Zettlemoyer 2013).

Examples of work aimed at broader linguistic coverage are Johan Bos' Boxer project (Bos 2008), Lewis & Steedman's (2013) CCG-Distributional system, James Allen et al.'s (2013) work on extracting an OWL-DL verb ontology from WordNet, and Draicchio et al.'s (2013) FRED system for mapping from NL to OWL ontology. Boxer[2] is highly developed, but interpretations are limited to FOL, so that the kinds of general quantification, reification and modification that pervade ordinary language cannot be adequately captured. The CCG-Distributional approach combines logical and distributional semantics in an interesting way, but apart from the FOL limitation, the induced cluster-based predicates lose distinctions such as that between *town* and *country* or between *elected to* and *ran for*. As such, the system is applicable to (soft) entailment verification, but probably not to reasoning. A major limitation of mapping natural language to OWL-DL is that the assertion component of the latter is essentially limited to atomic predications and their negations, so that ordinary statements such as *Most students who passed the AI exam also passed the theory exam*, or *If Kim and Sandy get divorced, then Kim will probably get custody of their children*, cannot be represented, let alone reasoned with.

7. Concluding thoughts

The history of research in natural language understanding shows two seemingly divergent trends: One is the attempt to faithfully capture the logical form of natural language sentences, and to study entailment relations based on such forms. The other is the effort to map language onto preexisting, schematic knowledge structures of some sort, intended as a basis for understanding and inference – these might be FrameNet-like or Minsky-like frames, concepts in a description logic, Schankian scripts, general plans as understood in AI, Pustejovskyan telic event schemas, or something similar. Both perspectives seem to have compelling merits, and this leads us to suppose that deep understanding may indeed require both surface representations and schematic representations, where surface representations can be viewed as concise abstractions from, or summaries of, schema instances or (for generic statements) of the schemas themselves. But where we differ from most approaches is that we would want both levels of representation to support inference. The surface level should support at least Natural-Logic-like entailment inference, along with inference chaining – for which EL and EPILOG are well-suited. The schematic level would support "reasonable" (or default) expectations based on familiar patterns of events, actions, or relationships. Further, the schematic level should itself allow for language-like expressiveness in the specification of roles, steps, goals, or other components, which might again be abstractions from more basic schemas. In other words, we envisage hierarchically organized schemas whose constituents are expressed in a language like EL and allow for EPILOG-like inference. We see the acquisition of such schemas as the most pressing need in machine understanding. Without them, we are limited to either narrow or shallow understanding.

[2] www.meaningfactory.com/bos/pubs/Bos2008STEP2.pdf

Acknowledgements

This work was supported by NSF grant IIS-0916599 and a subcontract to ONR STTR N00014-10-M-0297. The comments of the anonymous referees helped to improve the paper.

References

J. Allen, J. Orfan, W. de Beaumont, C. M. Teng, L. Galescu, M. Swift, 2013. Automatically deriving event ontologies for a commonsense knowledge base. *10th Int. Conf. on Computational Semantics (IWCS 2013)*, Potsdam, Germany, March 19-22.

Y. Artzi and L. Zettlemoyer, 2011. Bootstrapping Semantic Parsers from Conversations. *Empirical Methods in Natural Language Processing (EMNLP)*, Edinburgh, UK.

Y. Artzi and L. Zettlemoyer, 2013. Weakly supervised learning of semantic parsers for mapping instructions to actions. In *Trans. of the Assoc. for Computational Linguistics (TACL)*.

J. Berant, A. Chou, R. Frostig, P. Liang, 2013. Semantic parsing on Freebase from question-answer pairs.

Empirical Methods in Natural Language Processing (EMNLP), Seattle, WA.

J. Bos, 2008. Wide-coverage semantic analysis with Boxer. In J. Bos and R. Delmonte (eds.), *Semantics in Text Processing. STEP 2008 Conference Proceedings*. Research in Computational Semantics, College Publications, 277–286.

F. Draicchio, A. Gangemi, V. Presutti, and A.G. Nuzzolese, 2013. FRED: From natural language text to RDF and OWL in one click. In P. Cimiano et al. (eds.). *ESWC 2013, LNCS 7955*, Springer, 263-267.

R. Ge and R. J. Mooney, 2009. Learning a Compositional Semantic Parser using an Existing Syntactic Parser, In *Proceedings of the ACL-IJCNLP 2009*, Suntec, Singapore.

J. Gordon, 2014. Inferential Commonsense Knowledge from Text. Ph.D. Thesis, Department of Computer Science, University of Rochester, Rochester, NY. Available at http://www.cs.rochester.edu/u/jgordon/.

J. Gordon and L. K. Schubert, 2010. Quantificational sharpening of commonsense knowledge. *Common Sense Knowledge Symposium (CSK-10)*, AAAI 2010 Fall Symposium Series, Arlington, VA.

T. M. Howard, S. Tellex, and N. Roy, 2013. A Natural Language Planner Interface for Mobile Manipulators. *30th Int. Conf. on Machine Learning*, Atlanta, GA, JMLR: W&CP volume 28.

C. H. Hwang and L. K. Schubert, 1994. Interpreting tense, aspect, and time adverbials: a compositional, unified approach. D. M. Gabbay and H. J. Ohlbach (eds.), *Proc. of the 1st Int. Conf. on Temporal Logic*, Bonn, Germany, Springer, 238–264.

T. Kwiatkowski, E. Choi, Y. Artzi, and L. Zettlemoyer, 2013. Scaling semantic parsers with on-the-fly ontology matching. *Empirical Methods in Natural Language Processing (EMNLP)*, Seattle, WA.

T. Kwiatkowski, L. Zettlemoyer, S. Goldwater, and M. Steedman, 2011. Lexical generalization in CCG grammar induction for semantic parsing. *Empirical Methods in Natural Language Processing (EMNLP)*, Edinburgh, UK.

M. Lewis and M. Steedman, 2013. Combined distributional and logical semantics. *Trans. of the Assoc. for Computational Linguistics 1*, 179–192.

P. Liang, M. Jordan, and D. Klein, 2011. Learning dependency-based compositional semantics. *Conf. of the Assoc. for Computational Linguistics (ACL)*, Portland, OR.

B. MacCartney and C. D. Manning, 2009. An extended model of natural logic. *8th Int. Conf. on Computational Semantics (IWCS-8)*, Tilburg University, Netherlands. Assoc. for Computational Linguistics (ACL), Stroudsberg, PA.

W. H. McGuffey, 2005 (original edition 1879). *McGuffey's First Eclectic Reader*. John Wiley and Sons, New York.

F. Morbini and L. K. Schubert, 2011. Metareasoning as an integral part of commonsense and autocognitive reasoning. In M.T. Cox and A. Raja (eds.), *Metareasoning: Thinking about Thinking*, Ch. 17. MIT Press, Cambridge, MA, 267–282.

F. Morbini & Schubert, 2009. Evaluation of Epilog: A reasoner for Episodic Logic. Commonsense'09, June 1-3, Toronto, Canada. Available at http://commonsensereasoning.org/2009/papers.html.

H. Poon, 2013. Grounded unsupervised semantic parsing. *51st Ann. Meet. of the Assoc. for Computational Linguistics (ACL)*, Sofia, Bulgaria.

A. Purtee and L. K. Schubert, 2012. TTT: A tree transduction language for syntactic and semantic processing. *EACL 2012 Workshop on Applications of Tree Automata Techniques in Natural Language Processing (ATANLP 2012)*, Avignon, France.

L. K. Schubert, to appear. NLog-like inference and commonsense reasoning. In A. Zaenen, V. de Paiva and C. Condoravdi (eds.), *Semantics for Textual Inference*, CSLI Publications. Available at http://www.cs.rochester.edu/u/schubert/papers/nlog-like-inference12.pdf.

L. K. Schubert, 2000. The situations we talk about. In J. Minker (ed.), *Logic-Based Artificial Intelligence*, Kluwer, Dortrecht, 407–439.

L. K. Schubert and C. H. Hwang, 2000. Episodic Logic meets Little Red Riding Hood: A comprehensive, natural representation for language understanding. In L. Iwanska and S.C. Shapiro (eds.), *Natural Language Processing and Knowledge Representation: Language for Knowledge and Knowledge for Language*. MIT/AAAI Press, Menlo Park, CA, and Cambridge, MA, 111–174.

L. K. Schubert and F. J. Pelletier, 1982. From English to logic: Context-free computation of 'conventional' logical translations. *Am. J. of Computational Linguistics 8*, 27–44. Reprinted in B.J. Grosz, K. Sparck Jones, and B.L. Webber (eds.), *Readings in Natural Language Processing*, Morgan Kaufmann, Los Altos, CA, 1986, 293-311.

S. Tellex, T. Kollar, S. Dickerson, M. R. Walter, A. G. Banerjee, S. Teller, and N. Roy, 2011. Understanding natural language commands for robotic navigation and mobile manipulation. *Nat. Conf. on Artificial Intelligence (AAAI 2011)*, San Francisco, CA.

B. Van Durme and L. K. Schubert, 2008. Open knowledge extraction through compositional language processing. *Symposium on Semantics in Systems for Text Processing (STEP 2008)*, Venice, Italy.

On maximum spanning DAG algorithms for semantic DAG parsing

Natalie Schluter
Department of Computer Science
School of Technology, Malmö University
Malmö, Sweden
natalie.schluter@mah.se

Abstract

Consideration of the decoding problem in semantic parsing as finding a maximum spanning DAG of a weighted directed graph carries many complexities that haven't been fully addressed in the literature to date, among which are its actual appropriateness for the decoding task in semantic parsing, not to mention an explicit proof of its complexity (and its approximability). In this paper, we consider the objective function for the maximum spanning DAG problem, and what it means in terms of decoding for semantic parsing. In doing so, we give anecdotal evidence against its use in this task. In addition, we consider the only graph-based maximum spanning DAG approximation algorithm presented in the literature (without any approximation guarantee) to date and finally provide an approximation guarantee for it, showing that it is an $O(\frac{1}{n})$ factor approximation algorithm, where n is the size of the digraph's vertex set.

1 Introduction

Recent research in semantic parsing has moved attention towards recovering labeled digraph representations of the semantic relations corresponding to the linguistic agendas across a number of theories where simple tree representations are claimed not to be expressive enough to capture sentential meaning. As digraph structures presented in predominant semantic graph databases are mainly acyclic, the semantic parsing problem has sometimes become associated with a maximum spanning directed acyclic graph (MSDAG) decoding problem (McDonald and Pereira, 2006; Sagae and Tsujii, 2008; Titov et al., 2009), in analogy and perhaps as a generalisation of the maximum spanning tree decoding problem for syntactic dependency parsing.

The appropriateness of finding the MSDAG in decoding for semantic parsing has, however, never been fully motivated, and in fact carries more complexities than that of maximum spanning tree (MST) decoding for syntactic parsing. In this paper, we discuss the appropriateness of MSDAG decoding in semantic parsing, considering the possible objective functions and whether they match our linguistic goals for the decoding process. Our view is that they probably do not, in general.

In addition to the problem of not being sufficiently synchronised with our linguistic intuitions for the semantic parsing decoding problem, the MSDAG problem itself carries with it its own complexities, which are still in the process of becoming more understood in the algorithms research community. McDonald and Pereira (2006) claim that the MSDAG problem is **NP**-hard, citing (Heckerman et al., 1995); however, there is no MSDAG problem in this latter work, and no explicit reduction to any problem presented in (Heckerman et al., 1995) has been published to date. We point out that Schluter (submitted) explicitly provides a linear reduction to MSDAG from the problem of finding a minimum weighted directed multicut (IDMC), showing MSDAG's **NP**-hardness; this reduction also yields a result on the approximability of MSDAG, namely that it is **APX**-hard. We show in this paper that the approximation algorithm presented without any approximation guarantee in (McDonald and Pereira, 2006) is, in fact, a $O(\frac{1}{n})$ factor approximation algorithm, where n is the size of the graphs vertex set. This is not particularly surprising given the problem's **APX**-hardness.

Following some preliminaries on weighted digraphs (Section 2), we make the MSDAG problem precise through a discussion of the objective function in question and briefly question this ob-

Proceedings of the ACL 2014 Workshop on Semantic Parsing, pages 61–65,
Baltimore, Maryland USA, June 26 2014.

jective function with respect to decoding in semantic parsing (Section 3). Finally, we discuss the only other graph-based (approximation) algorithm in the literature and prove its approximation guarantee (Section 4), followed by some brief conclusions (Section 5).

2 Preliminaries

A *directed graph* (or *digraph*) G is a pair (V, E) where V is the set of *nodes* and E is the set of *(directed) edges*. $E \subset V \times V$ is a set of ordered pairs of vertices. For $u, v \in V$, if $(u, v) \in E$, then we say there is an "edge from u to v". If there is any confusion over the digraph we are referring to, then we disambiguate by using the notation $G := (E(G), V(G))$.

If all edges $e \in E(G)$ are associated with a real number, a weight $w : E(G) \to \mathbb{R}$, then we call the digraph *weighted*. In this paper, all digraphs are weighted and weights are positive.

For a subset of edges U of a weighted digraph, we set $w(U) := \sum_{e \in U} w(e)$. Similarly, for a weighted digraph G, we set $w(G) := \sum_{e \in E(G)} w(e)$.

We denote the size of a set S, by $|S|$.

For $G = (V, E)$, let $u_1, \ldots, u_k \in V$ and $(u_i, u_{i+1}) \in E$, for each $i \in [k-1]$, then we say that there is *path* (also *directed path*, or *dipath*) of length $(k-1)$ from u_1 to u_k in G. If also $(u_k, u_1) \in E$, then we say that $u_1, u_2, \ldots, u_k, u_1$ is a *cycle* of length k in G.

A *directed acyclic graph* (DAG) is a directed graph with no cycles. There is a special kind of DAG, which has a special node called a *root* with no incoming edges and in which there is a unique path from the root to all nodes; this is called a *tree*.

Finally, a *tournament* is a digraph in which all pairs of vertices are connected by exactly one edge. If, in addition, the edges are weighted, then we call the digraph a *weighted tournament*.

3 Objective functions for finding an MSDAG of a digraph

We first make precise the objective function for the MSDAG problem, by considering two separate objective functions, one additive and one multiplicative, over the weights of edges in the optimal solution:

$$D^* := \underset{D \text{ a spanning DAG of } G}{\arg\max} \sum_{e \in E(D)} w(e), \text{ and} \quad (1)$$

$$D^* := \underset{D \text{ a spanning DAG of } G}{\arg\max} \prod_{e \in E(D)} w(e). \quad (2)$$

Maximising Equation (2) amounts to concurrently minimising the number of edges of weight less than 1 in the optimal solution and maximising the number of edges of weight at least 1. In fact, if all edge weights are less than 1, then this problem reduces to finding the MST. However, the objective in semantic parsing in adopting the MSDAG problem for decoding is to increase power from finding only MSTs. Therefore, this version of the problem is not the subject of this paper. If a graph has even one edge of weight greater than 1, then all edges of lesser weights should be discarded, and for the remaining subgraph, maximising Equations (1) or (2) is equivalent.

Maximising Equation (1) is complex and under certain restrictions on edge weights may optimise for simply the number of edges (subject to being a DAG). For example, if the difference between any two edge weights is less than $\frac{1}{|E(G)|} \times w(e)$ for the smallest weighted e in $E(G)$, then the problem reduces to finding the spanning DAG with the greatest number of edges, as shown by Proposition 1.

Proposition 1. *Let G be a weighted digraph, with minimum edge weight M. Suppose the difference in weight between any two edges of G is at most $\frac{1}{|E(G)|} \times M$. Then an MSDAG for G maximises the number of edges of any spanning DAG for G.*

Proof. Suppose D_1, D_2 are spanning DAGs for G, such that (without loss of generality) $|E(D_1)| = |E(D_2)| + 1$, but that D_2 is an MSDAG and that D_1 is not. We derive the following contradiction.

$$\begin{aligned} w(D_2) &= \sum_{e \in E(D_2)} w(e) \\ &\leq |E(D_2)| \cdot M + |E(D_2)| \cdot \left(\frac{1}{|E(G)|} \cdot M\right) \\ &< |E(D_2)| \cdot M + M \\ &= |E(D_1)| \cdot M \\ &\leq \sum_{e \in E(D_2)} w(e) \\ &= w(D_1) \end{aligned}$$

□

Admittedly, for arbitrary edge weights, the relation between the sum of edge weights and number of edges is more intricate, and it is this problem that we refer to as the MSDAG problem in this paper. However, the maximisation of the number of edges in the MSDAG does play a role when using Equation (1) as the objective function, and this may be inappropriate for decoding in semantic parsing.

3.1 Two linguistic issues of in MSDAG decoding for semantic parsing

We can identify two important related issues against linguistic motivation for the use of MSDAG algorithms in decoding for semantic parsing. The first problem is inherited from that of the arc-factored model in syntactic parsing, and the second problem is due to MSDAGs constrained maximisation of edges discussed above.

In the arc-factored syntactic parsing paradigm, it was shown that the MST algorithm could be used for exact inference (McDonald et al., 2005). However, one problem with this paradigm was that edges of the inferred solution did not linguistically constrain each other. So, for example, a verb can be assigned two separate subject dependents, which is linguistically absurd. Use of the MSDAG algorithm in semantic parsing corresponds, in fact, to a generalisation of the arc-factored syntactic parsing paradigm to semantic parsing. As such, the problem of a lack of linguistic constraints among edges is inherited by the arc-factored semantic parsing paradigm.

However, MSDAG decoding for semantic parsing suffers from a further problem. In MST decoding, the only constraint is really that the output should have a tree structure; this places a precise restriction on the number of edges in the output (i.e., $n-1$), unlike for MSDAGs. From our discussion above, we know that the MSDAG problem is closely related to a constrained maximisation of edges. In particular, a candidate solution s to the problem that is not optimal in terms of total weight may, however, be linguistically optimal; adding further edges to s would increase weight, but may be linguistically undesirable.

Consider the tree at the top of Figure 1, for the example *John loves Mary*. In decoding, this tree could be our linguistic optimal, however according to our additive objective function, it is more likely for us to obtain either of the bottom DAGs, which is clearly not what is wanted in semantic parsing.

4 Related Research and an Approximation Guarantee

The only algorithm presented to date for MSDAG is an approximation algorithm proposed by Mc-

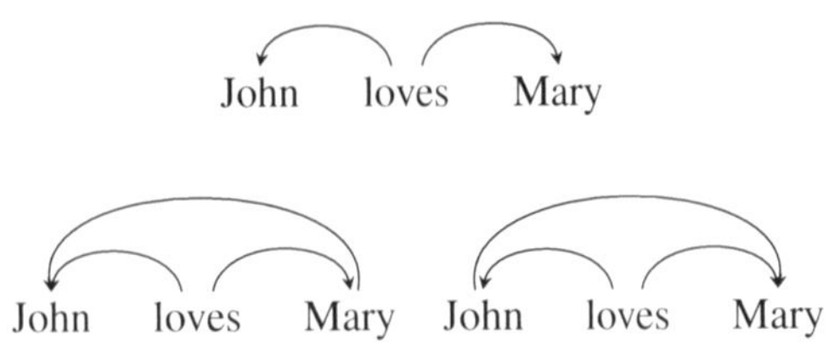

Figure 1: Possible spanning DAGs for *John loves Mary*.

Donald and Pereira (2006), given without any approximation guarantee. The algorithm first constructs an MST of the weighted digraph, and then greedily attempts to add remaining edges to the MST in order of descending weight, so long as no cycle is introduced. Only part of this algorithm is greedy, so we will refer to it as **`semi-greedy-MSDAG`**. Given the fact that MSDAG is **APX**-hard (Schluter, submitted), the following approximation guarantee is not surprising.

Theorem 2. ***`semi-greedy-MSDAG`*** *is an* $O(\frac{1}{n})$ *factor approximation algorithm for MSDAG.*

Proof. We separate the proof into two parts. In Part 1, we first consider an easy worst case scenario for an upper bound on the error for **`semi-greedy-MSDAG`**, without any consideration for whether such a graph actually exists. Following this in Part 2, we construct a family of graphs to show that this bound is tight (i.e., that the algorithm exhibits worst imaginable behaviour for this family of graphs).

Part 1. For G a digraph, let D be the output of **`semi-greedy-MSDAG`** on G, and D^* be an MSDAG for G. The worst case is (bounded by the case) where the algorithm finds an MST T^* for G but then cannot introduce any extra edges to obtain a spanning DAG of higher weight, because the addition of any extra edges would induce a cycle. For G's nodes, we suppose that $|V(G)| > 3$. For edges, we suppose that all the edges in T^* have equally the largest weight, say w_{max}, of any edge in $E(G)$, and that all other edges in $E(G)$ have weight $O(w_{max})$. We can do this, because it gives an advantage to T^*.

We suppose also that the underlying undirected graph of G is complete and that the true MSDAG for G is $D^* := (V(G), E(G) - E(T^*))$.

This clearly must be the worst imaginable case: that T^* shares no edges with D^*, but that D^* contains every other possible edge in the graph, with the weight of every edge in D^* being at most the weight of the maximum weighted edge of those of T^* (remember we are trying to favour T^*). No other imaginable case could introduce more edges to D^* without inducing a cycle. So, for all G,

$$w(D^*) = O\left(\frac{(n-1)^2 \cdot w_{max}}{2}\right) = O(n^2 \cdot w_{max}),$$

and we had that $w(T^*) = w(D) = O(n \cdot w_{max})$. So at very worst, **semi-greedy-MSDAG** finds a spanning DAG D of weight within $O(\frac{1}{n})$ of the optimal.

Part 2. We now show that this bound is tight. We construct a family of graphs $G_n = (V_n, E_n)$ as follows. $V_n := \{v_0, v_1, v_2, \ldots, v_n\}$, with $n > 3$, and we suppose that n is even. Let $c \in \mathbb{R}$ be some constant such that $c > 3$. We place the following edges in E_n:

(E1) (v_i, v_{i+1}) of weight c for all $i \in \{0, \ldots, n-1\}$ into E_n, creating a path from v_0 to v_n of length n where every edge has weight c, and

(E2) (v_i, v_j) of weight $c-1$ for all $j \in \{2, i-1\}$, $i \in \{2, \ldots, n\}$.

So, in addition to the path defined by the edges in (E1), $G_n - \{v_0\}$ contains a weighted tournament on $n-1$ nodes, such that if $j < i$, then there is an edge from i to j.

Let us denote the MST of G_n by T_n^* and the maximal spanning tree obtainable by **semi-greedy-MSDAG**, by D_n. We will show that the (unique) MSDAG of G_n is the graph D_n^* that we construct below.

It is easy to see that the MST T_n^* of G_n consists of the edges in (E1), and that no further edges can be added to T_n^* without creating a cycle. So, $D_n = T_n^*$.

On the other hand, we claim that there is a unique D_n^* consisting of:

1. the edge (v_0, v_1),
2. the edges (v_{2i-1}, v_{2i}) for all $i \in \{1, \ldots, n/2\}$ into $E(D_n^*)$, that is every second edge in the path described in (E1), and
3. all the edges from (E2) except for (v_{2i}, v_{2i-1}) for all $i \in \{1, \ldots, n/2\}$.

We can easily see that D_n^* is at least maximal. The only edges not in D_n^* are ones that are parallel to other edges. So, introducing any other edge from (E2) would mean removing an edge from (E1), which would decrease D_n^*'s overall weight. Moreover, notice that introducing any other edge from (E1), say (v_{k-1}, v_k) would require removing two edges (from (E2)), either (v_k, v_{k-1}) and (v_{k+1}, v_{k-1}) or (v_k, v_{k-1}) and (v_k, v_{k+1}), to avoid cycles in D_n^*, but this also decreases overall weight. We extend these two simple facts in the remainder of the proof, showing that D^*, in addition to being maximal, is also a global maximum.

We prove the result by induction on n (with n even), that D_n^* is the MSDAG for G_n. We take $n = 4$ as our base case.

For G_4 (see Figure 2), $E(G_4) - E(D_4^*)$ contains only three edges: the edge (v_2, v_3) of weight c and the edges (v_4, v_3) and (v_2, v_1) of weight $(c-1)$. Following the same principles above, adding the edge (v_2, v_1) would entail removing an edge of higher weight; the same is true of adding the edge (v_4, v_3). No further edges in either case could be added to make up this difference and achieve greater weight than D_4^*. So the only option is to add the edge (v_2, v_3). However, this would entail removing either the two edges (v_3, v_2) and (v_4, v_2) or (v_3, v_2) and (v_3, v_4) from D_4^*, both of which actions results in lower overall weight.

Now suppose D_{n-2}^* is optimal (for $n \geq 6$, n even). We show that this implies D_n^* is optimal (with n even). Consider the two subgraphs G_{n-2} and H of G_n induced by the subsets of $V(G_n)$, $V(G_{n-2}) = \{v_0, \ldots, v_{n-2}\}$ and $V(H) := \{v_{n-1}, v_n\}$ respectively (so $H = (V(H), \{(v_{n-1}, v_n), (v_{n-1}, v_n)\})$). We are assuming that the MSDAG of G_{n-2} is D_{n-2}^*. Moreover, the MSDAG of H is a single edge, $D_H := (V(H), \{(v_{n-1}, v_n)\})$.

D_n^* includes the MSDAGs (D_{n-2}^* and D_H) of these two digraphs, so for these parts of D_n^*, we have reached an upper bound for optimality. Now we consider the optimal way to connect D_{n-2}^* and D_H to create D_n^*.

Let C denote the set of edges in G_n which connect D_H to G_{n-2} and vice versa. $C = \{(v_{n-2}, v_{n-1})\} \cup \{(u_n, u_i) \mid 1 \leq i < n\} \cup \{(u_{n-1}, u_i) \mid 1 \leq i < n-1\}$. Note that the only edge from C not included in D_n^* is $e_C := (v_{n-2}, v_{n-1})$. By the discussion above, we know that including e_C would mean excluding two other edges from C of weight at least $(c-1)$, which cannot be optimal. Therefore D_n^* must be optimal.

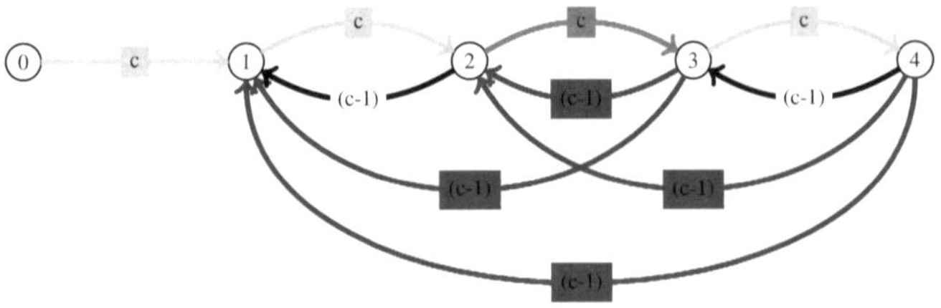

Figure 2: G_4, with D_4^* in blue and green and T_4^* in red and green.

So we have constructed a family of graphs G_n where $w(D_n) = w(T_n^*) = nc$ and

$$w(D_n^*) = \left(\sum_{i=0}^{n-1} i(c-1) + (n \cdot c)\right) - (\frac{n}{2} \cdot c) = \frac{n(n-1)}{2}(c-1) - \frac{n}{2} \cdot c.$$

This completes the proof that **semi-greedy-MSDAG** is an $O\left(\frac{nc}{\frac{n(n-1)}{2}(c-1) - \frac{n}{2} \cdot c}\right) = O(\frac{1}{n})$ factor approximation algorithm for MSDAG. □

Now let us consider the version of the statement of the MSDAG problem that, rather than maximising the weight of a spanning DAG D^* of a weighted digraph G, looks to minimise the weight of the set C^* of edges that must be removed from G in order for $G - C^*$ to be an MSDAG for G. Clearly these problems are identical. We refer to the minimisation version of the statement as $MSDAG^C$, and to C^* as the complement (in G) of the MSDAG $D^* := G - C^*$. Also, let **semi-greedy-MSDAG**^{C} be the same algorithm as **semi-greedy-MSDAG** except that it outputs C^* rather than D^*.

Using the same graphs and proof structure as in the proof of Theorem 2, the following theorem can be shown.

Theorem 3. ***semi-greedy-MSDAG***^{C} *is an $O(n)$ factor approximation algorithm for MSDAG^C.*

5 Conclusions and Open Questions

This paper provides some philosophical and mathematical foundations for the MSDAG problem as decoding in semantic parsing. We have put forward the view that the objective in semantic parsing is not in fact to find the MSDAG, however it remains open as to whether this mismatch can be tolerated, given empirical evidence of MSDAG decoding's utility in semantic parsing. We have also pointed to an explicit proof of the **APX**-hardness (that of (Schluter, submitted)) of MSDAG and given an approximation guarantee of the only published approximation algorithm for this problem.

In particular, Schluter (submitted) provides an approximation preserving reduction from MSDAG^C to IDMC. Moreover, the best known approximation ratio for IDMC is $O(n^{\frac{11}{23}})$ (Agarwal et al., 2007), which yields a better (in terms of worst case error) approximation algorithm for MSDAG^C. An interesting open problem would compare these two decoding approximation algorithms empirically for semantic parsing decoding and in terms of expected performance (or error) both in general as well as specifically for semantic parsing decoding.

References

Amit Agarwal, Noga Alon, and Moses Charikar. 2007. Improved approximation for directed cut problems. In *Proceedings of STOC*, San Diego, CA.

D. Heckerman, D. Geiger, and D. M. Chickering. 1995. Learning bayesian networks: The combination of knowledge and statistical data. Technical report, Microsoft Research. MSR-TR-94-09.

Ryan McDonald and Fernando Pereira. 2006. Online learning of approximate dependency parsing algorithms. In *Proc. of EACL*, pages 81–88.

R. McDonald, F. Pereira, K. Ribarov, and J. Haji. 2005. Non-projective dependency parsing using spanning tree algorithms. In *Proc. of HLT-EMNLP*, pages 523–530, Vancouver, BC, Canada.

Kenji Sagae and Jun'ichi Tsujii. 2008. Shift-reduce dependency dag parsing. In *22nd International Conference on Computational Linguistics (Coling 2008)*, Manchester, UK.

Natalie Schluter. submitted. On the complexity of finding a maximum spanning dag and other dag parsing related restrictions.

Ivan Titov, James Henderson, Paola Merlo, and Gabrielle Musillo. 2009. Online graph planarization for synchronous parsing of semantic and syntactic dependencies. In *Proceedings of IJCAI 2009*, pages 1562–1567.

Intermediary Semantic Representation through Proposition Structures

Gabriel Stanovsky*, **Jessica Ficler***, **Ido Dagan**, **Yoav Goldberg**
Computer Science Department, Bar-Ilan University
*Both authors equally contributed to this paper
{gabriel.satanovsky,jessica.ficler,yoav.goldberg}@gmail.com
dagan@cs.biu.ac.il

Abstract

We propose an intermediary-level semantic representation, providing a higher level of abstraction than syntactic parse trees, while not committing to decisions in cases such as quantification, grounding or verb-specific roles assignments. The proposal is centered around the proposition structure of the text, and includes also implicit propositions which can be inferred from the syntax but are not transparent in parse trees, such as copular relations introduced by appositive constructions. Other benefits over dependency-trees are explicit marking of logical relations between propositions, explicit marking of multi-word predicate such as light-verbs, and a consistent representation for syntactically-different but semantically-similar structures. The representation is meant to serve as a useful input layer for semantic-oriented applications, as well as to provide a better starting point for further levels of semantic analysis such as semantic-role-labeling and semantic-parsing.

1 Introduction

Parsers for semantic formalisms (such as Neo-davidsonian (Artzi and Zettlemoyer, 2013) and DRT (Kamp, 1988)) take unstructured natural language text as input, and output a complete semantic representation, aiming to capture the meaning conveyed by the text. We suggest that this task may be effectively separated into a sequential combination of two different tasks. The first of these tasks is *syntactic abstraction* over phenomena such as expression of tense, negation, modality, and passive versus active voice, which are all either expressed or implied from syntactic structure. The second task is *semantic interpretation* over the syntactic abstraction, deriving quantification, grounding, etc. Current semantic parsers (such as Boxer (Bos, 2008)) tackle these tasks simultaneously, mixing syntactic and semantic issues in a single framework. We believe that separating semantic parsing into two well defined tasks will help to better target and identify challenges in syntactic and semantic domains. Challenges which are often hidden due to the one-step architecture of current parsers.

Many of today's semantic parsers, and semantic applications in general, leverage dependency parsing (De Marneffe and Manning, 2008a) as an abstraction layer, since it directly represents syntactic dependency relations between predicates and arguments. Some systems exploit Semantic Role Labeling (SRL) (Carreras and M'arquez, 2005), where predicate-argument relationships are captured at a thematic (rather than syntactic) level, though current SRL technology is less robust and accurate for open domains than syntactic parsing. While dependency structures and semantic roles capture much of the proposition structure of sentences, there are substantial aspects which are not covered by these representations and therefore need to be handled by semantic applications on their own (or they end up being ignored).

Such aspects, as detailed in Section 3, include propositions which are not expressed directly as such but are rather implied by syntactic structure, like nominalizations, appositions and premodifying adjectives. Further, the same proposition structure may be expressed in many different ways by the syntactic structure, forcing systems to recognize this variability and making the task of recognizing semantic roles harder. Other aspects not addressed by common representations include explicit marking of links between propositions within a sentence, which affect their assertion or truth status, and the recognition of multi-word predicates (e.g., considering "take a deci-

Proceedings of the ACL 2014 Workshop on Semantic Parsing, pages 66–70,
Baltimore, Maryland USA, June 26 2014.

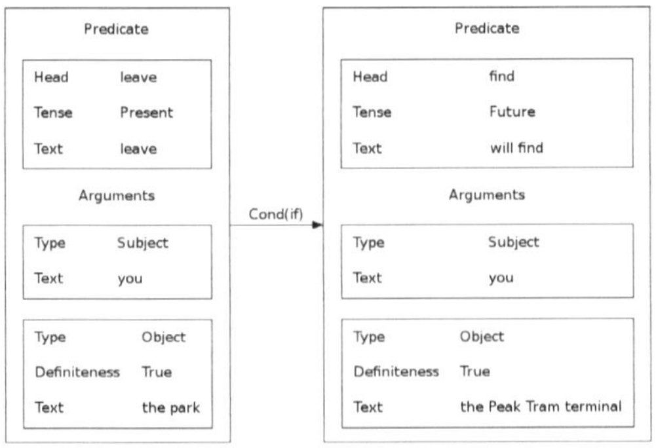

Figure 1: Proposed representation for the sentence: "If you leave the park, you will find the Peak Tram terminal"

sion" as a single predicate, rather than considering decision as an argument).

In this position paper we propose an intermediary representation level for the first syntactic abstraction phase described above, intended to replace syntactic parsing as a more abstract representation layer. It is designed to capture the full proposition structure which is expressed, either explicitly or implicitly, by the syntactic structure of sentences. Thus, we aim to both extract implicit propositions as well as to abstract away syntactic variations which yield the same proposition structure. At the same time, we aim to remain at a representation level that corresponds to syntactic properties and relationships, while avoiding semantic interpretations, to be targeted by systems implementing the further step of semantic interpretation, as discussed above.

In addition, we suggest our representation as a useful input for semantic applications which need to recognize the proposition structure of sentences in order to identify targeted information, such as Question Answering(QA), Information Extraction (IE) and multidocument summarization. We expect that our representation may be more useful in comparison with current popular use of dependency parsing, in such applications.

2 Representation Scheme

Our representation is centered around *propositions*, where a proposition is a statement for which a truth-value can be assigned. We propose to represent sentences as a set of inter-linked propositions. Each proposition is composed of one predicate and a set of arguments. An example representation can be seen in Figure 1. Predicates are usually centered around verbs, and we consider multi-word verbs (e.g., "take apart") as single predicates. Both the predicates and arguments are represented as sets of feature-value pairs. Each argument is marked with a relation to its predicate, and the same argument can appear in different propositions. The relation-set we use is syntactic in nature, including relations such as `Subject`, `Object`, and `Preposition_with`, in contrast to semantic relations such as `instrument`.

Canonical Representation The same proposition can be realized syntactically in many forms. An important goal of our proposal is abstracting over idiosyncrasies in the syntactic structure and presenting unified structures when possible. We canonicalize on two levels:

- We canonicalize each predicate and argument by representing each predicate as its main lemma, and indicating other aspects of the predication (e.g., tense, negation and time) as features; Similarly, we mark arguments with features such as definiteness and plurality.

- We canonicalize the argument structure by abstracting away over word order and phenomena such as topicalization and passive/active voice, and present a unified representation in terms of the argument roles (so that, for example, in the sentence "the door was opened" the argument "door" will receive the `object` role, with the passive being indicated as a feature of the predicate).

Relations Between Propositions Some propositions must be interpreted taking into account their relations to other propositions. These include conditionals (*"if congress does nothing, President Bush will have won"* (**wsj_0112**)); temporal relations (*"UAL's announcement came after the market closed yesterday"*(**wsj_0112**)); and conjunctions (*"They operate ships and banks."*(**wsj_0083**)).

We model such relations as typed links between extracted propositions. Figure 1 presents an example of handling a conditional relation: the dependence between the propositions is made explicit by the `Cond(if)` relation.

3 Implicit Propositions

Crucially, our proposal aims to capture not only explicit but also implicit propositions – propositions that can be inferred from the syntactic structure but which are not explicitly marked in syntactic dependency trees, as we elaborate below. Some of these phenomena are relatively easy to address by post-processing over syntactic parsers, and could thus be included in a first implementation that produces our proposed representations. Other phenomena are more subtle and would require further research, yet they seem important while not being addressed by current techniques. The syntactic structures giving rise to implicit propositions include:

Copular sentences such as *"This is not a trivial issue."* **(wsj_0108)** introduces a proposition by linking between a non-verbal predicate and its argument. We represent this by making *"not a trivial issue"* a predicate, and *"this"* an argument of type *Predication*.

Appositions, we distinguish between co-reference and predicative appositions. In **Co-reference indication appositions** (*"The company, Random House, doesn't report its earnings."* (adaption of **wsj_0111**)) we produce a proposition to indicate the co-reference between two lexical items. Other propositions relating to the entity use the main clause as the referent for this entity. In this example, we will produce:
1. Random House == the company.
2. The company doesn't report its earnings.

In **Predicative appositions** (*"Pierre Vinken, 61 years old, will join the board as a nonexecutive director Nov. 29."* **(wsj_0001)**) an apposition is used in order to convey knowledge about an entity. In our representation this will produce:
1. Pierre Vinken is 61 years old (which is canonicalized to the representation of copular sentences)
2. Pierre Vinken will join the board as a nonexecutive director Nov. 29.

Adjectives, as in the sentence *"you emphasized the high prevalence of mental illness"* **(wsj_0105)**. Here an adjective is used to describe a definite subject and introduces another proposition, namely the high prevalence of mental illness.

Nominalizations, for instance in the sentence *"Googles acquisition of Waze occurred yesterday"*, introduce the implicit proposition that *"Google acquired Waze"*. Such propositions were studied and annotated in the NOMLEX (Macleod et al., 1998) and NOMBANK (Meyers et al., 2004) resources. It remains an open issue how to represent or distinguish cases in which nominalization introduce an underspecified proposition. For example, consider "dancing" in *"I read a book about dancing"*.

Possessives, such as *"John's book"* introduce the proposition that John has a book. Similarly, examples such as *"John's Failure"* combine a possessive construction with nominalization and introduce the proposition that John has failed.

Conjunctions - for example in *"They operate ships and banks."* **(wsj_0083)**, introduce several propositions in one sentence:
1. They operate ships
2. They operate banks
We mark that *they* co-refer to the same lexical unit in the original sentence. Such cases are already represented explicitly in the "collapsed" version of Stanford-dependencies (De Marneffe and Manning, 2008a).[1]

Implicit future tense indication, for instance in *"I'm going to vote for it"* **(wsj_0098)** and *"The economy is about to slip into recession."* **(wsj_0036)**, verbs like *"going to"* and *"about to"* are used as future-tense markers of the proposition following them, rather than predicates on their own. We represent these as a single predicate (*"vote"*) in which the tense is marked as a feature.[2]

Other phenomena, omitted for lack of space, include **propositional modifiers** (e.g., relative clause modifiers), **propositional arguments** (such as *"John asserted that he will go home"*), **conditionals**, and the canonicalization of **passive and active voice**.

4 Relation to Other Representations

Our proposed representation is intended to serve as a bridging layer between purely syntactic representations such as dependency trees, and semantic oriented applications. In particular, we explicitly represent many semantic relations expressed in a sentence that are not captured by contemporary proposition-directed semantic representations (Baker et al., 1998; Kingsbury and Palmer, 2003; Meyers et al., 2004; Carreras and Màrquez, 2005).

Compared to dependency-based representations such as Stanford-dependency trees (De Marneffe

[1] A case of conjunctions requiring special treatment is introduced by **reciprocals**, in which the entities roles are exchangeable. For example: *"John and Mary bet against each other on future rates"* (adaption of **wsj_0117**).

[2] Care needs to be taken to distinguish from cases such as *"going to Italy"* in which *"going to"* is not followed by a verbal predicate.

and Manning, 2008b), we abstract away over many syntactic details (e.g., the myriad of ways of expressing tense, negation and modality, or the difference between passive and active) which are not necessary for semantic interpretation and mark them instead using a unified set of features and argument types. We make explicit many relations that can be inferred from the syntax but which are not directly encoded in dependency relations. We directly connect predicates with all of their arguments in e.g., conjunctions and embedded constructions, and we do not commit to a tree structure. We also explicitly mark predicate and argument boundaries, and explicitly mark multi-word predicates such as light-verb constructions.

Compared to proposition-based semantic representations, we do not attempt to assign frame-specific thematic roles, nor do we attempt to disambiguate or interpret word meanings. We restrict ourselves to representing predicates by their (lemmatized) surface forms, and labeling arguments based on a "syntactic" role inventory, similar to the label-sets available in dependency representations. This design choice makes our representation much easier to assign automatically to naturally occurring text (perhaps pre-annotated using a syntactic parser) than it is to assign semantic roles. At the same time, as described in Section 3, we capture many relations that are currently not annotated in resources such as FrameNet, and provide a comprehensive set of propositions present in the sentence (either explicitly or implicitly) as well as the relations between them – an objective which is not trivial even when presented with full semantic representation.

Compared to more fine-grained semantic representations used in semantic-parsers (i.e. lambda-calculus (Zettlemoyer and Collins, 2005), neo-davidsonian semantics (Artzi and Zettlemoyer, 2013), DRT (Kamp, 1988) or the DCS representation of Liang (2011)), we do not attempt to tackle quantification, nor to ground the arguments and predicates to a concrete domain-model or ontology. These important tasks are orthogonal to our representation, and we believe that semantic-parsers can benefit from our proposal by using it as input in addition to or instead of the raw sentence text – quantification, binding and grounding are hard enough without needing to deal with the subtleties of syntax or the identification of implicit propositions.

5 Conclusion and Future Work

We proposed an intermediate semantic representation through proposition extraction, which captures both explicit and implicit propositions, while staying relatively close to the syntactic level. We believe that this kind of representation will serve not only as an advantageous input for semantically-centered applications, such as question answering, summarization and information extraction, but also serve as a rich representation layer that can be used as input for systems aiming to provide a finer level of semantic analysis, such as semantic-parsers.

We are currently at the beginning of our investigation. In the near future we plan to semi-automatically annotate the Penn Tree Bank (Marcus et al., 1993) with these structures, as well as to provide software for deriving (some of) the implicit and explicit annotations from automatically produced parse-trees. We believe such resources will be of immediate use to semantic-oriented applications. In the longer term, we plan to investigate dedicated algorithms for automatically producing such representation from raw text.

The architecture we describe can easily accommodate *additional layers of abstraction*, by encoding these layers as features of propositions, predicates or arguments. Such layers can include the marking of named entities, the truth status of propositions and author commitment.

In the current version *infinitive* constructions are treated as nested propositions, similar to their representation in syntactic parse trees. Providing a consistent, useful and transparent representation for infinitive constructions is a challenging direction for future research.

Other extensions of the proposed representation are also possible. One appealing direction is going beyond the sentence level and representing *discourse level relations*, including implied propositions and predicate - argument relationships expressed by discourse (Stern and Dagan, 2014; Ruppenhofer et al., 2010; Gerber and Chai, 2012). Such an extension may prove useful as an intermediary representation for parsers of semantic formalisms targeted at the discourse level (such as DRT).

6 Acknowledgments

This work was partially supported by the European Community's Seventh Framework Programme (FP7/2007-2013) under grant agreement no. 287923 (EXCITEMENT).

References

Yoav Artzi and Luke Zettlemoyer. 2013. Weakly supervised learning of semantic parsers for mapping instructions to actions. *Transactions of the Association for Computational Linguistics*, 1(1):49–62.

Collin F Baker, Charles J Fillmore, and John B Lowe. 1998. The berkeley framenet project. In *Proceedings of ACL*, pages 86–90. Association for Computational Linguistics.

Johan Bos. 2008. Wide-coverage semantic analysis with boxer. In *Proceedings of the 2008 Conference on Semantics in Text Processing*, pages 277–286. Association for Computational Linguistics.

Xavier Carreras and Lluís Màrquez. 2005. Introduction to the conll-2005 shared task: Semantic role labeling. In *Proceedings of CONLL*, pages 152–164.

Marie-Catherine De Marneffe and Christopher D Manning. 2008a. Stanford typed dependencies manual. Technical report, Stanford University.

Marie-Catherine De Marneffe and Christopher D Manning. 2008b. The stanford typed dependencies representation. In *Coling 2008: Proceedings of the workshop on Cross-Framework and Cross-Domain Parser Evaluation*, pages 1–8.

Matthew Gerber and Joyce Y Chai. 2012. Semantic role labeling of implicit arguments for nominal predicates. *Computational Linguistics*, 38(4):755–798.

Hans Kamp. 1988. Discourse representation theory. In *Natural Language at the computer*, pages 84–111. Springer.

Paul Kingsbury and Martha Palmer. 2003. Propbank: the next level of treebank. In *Proceedings of Treebanks and lexical Theories*, volume 3.

P. Liang, M. I. Jordan, and D. Klein. 2011. Learning dependency-based compositional semantics. In *Proceedings of ACL*, pages 590–599.

Catherine Macleod, Ralph Grishman, Adam Meyers, Leslie Barrett, and Ruth Reeves. 1998. Nomlex: A lexicon of nominalizations. In *Proceedings of EURALEX*, volume 98, pages 187–193.

Mitchell P Marcus, Mary Ann Marcinkiewicz, and Beatrice Santorini. 1993. Building a large annotated corpus of english: The penn treebank. *Computational linguistics*, 19(2):313–330.

Adam Meyers, Ruth Reeves, Catherine Macleod, Rachel Szekely, Veronika Zielinska, Brian Young, and Ralph Grishman. 2004. The nombank project: An interim report. In *HLT-NAACL 2004 workshop: Frontiers in corpus annotation*, pages 24–31.

Josef Ruppenhofer, Caroline Sporleder, Roser Morante, Collin Baker, and Martha Palmer. 2010. Semeval-2010 task 10: Linking events and their participants in discourse. In *Proceedings of the 5th International Workshop on Semantic Evaluation*, pages 45–50. Association for Computational Linguistics.

Asher Stern and Ido Dagan. 2014. Recognizing implied predicate-argument relationships in textual inference. In *Proceedings of ACL*. Association for Computational Linguistics.

Luke S. Zettlemoyer and Michael Collins. 2005. Learning to map sentences to logical form: Structured classification with probabilistic categorial grammars. In *UAI*, pages 658–666. AUAI Press.

Efficient Logical Inference for Semantic Processing

Ran Tian* **Yusuke Miyao** **Takuya Matsuzaki**
National Institute of Informatics, Japan
{tianran,yusuke,takuya-matsuzaki}@nii.ac.jp

Abstract

Dependency-based Compositional Semantics (DCS) provides a precise and expressive way to model semantics of natural language queries on relational databases, by simple dependency-like trees. Recently abstract denotation is proposed to enable generic logical inference on DCS. In this paper, we discuss some other possibilities to equip DCS with logical inference, and we discuss further on how logical inference can help textual entailment recognition, or other semantic precessing tasks.

1 Introduction

Dependency-based Compositional Semantics (DCS) was proposed as an interface for querying relational databases by natural language. It features DCS trees as semantic representation, with a structure similar to dependency trees. In its basic version, a node of a DCS tree indicates a table in the database, and an edge indicates a join relation. Both ends of an edge are labeled by a field of the corresponding table (Liang et al., 2011). However, when DCS is applied to logical inference on unrestricted texts, it is unrealistic to assume an explicit database, because we cannot prepare a database for everything in the world. For this reason, DCS trees are detached from any specific relational database, in a way that each node of a DCS tree indicates a content word in a sentence (thus no fixed set of possible word labels for a DCS tree node), and each edge indicates a semantic relation between two words. Labels on the two ends of an edge, initially indicating fields of tables in a database, are considered as semantic roles of the corresponding words. Abstract denotation is proposed to capture the meaning of this abstract version of DCS tree, and a textual inference system based on abstract denotation is built (Tian et al., 2014).

It is quite natural to apply DCS trees, a simple and expressive semantic representation, to textual inference; however the use of abstract denotations to convey logical inference is somehow unusual. There are two seemingly obvious way to equip DCS with logical inference: (i) at the tree level, by defining a set of logically sound transformations of DCS trees; or (ii) at the logic level, by converting DCS trees to first order predicate logic (FOL) formulas and then utilizing a theorem prover. For (i), it may not be easy to enumerate all types of logically sound transformations, but tree transformations can be seen as an approximation of logical inference. For (ii), abstract denotation is more efficient than FOL formula, because abstract denotation eliminates quantifiers and meanings of natural language texts can be represented by atomic sentences.

To elaborate the above discussion and to provide more topics to the literature, in this paper we discuss the following four questions: (§2) How well can tree transformation approximate logical inference? (§3) With rigorous inference on DCS trees, where does logic contribute in the system of Tian et al. (2014)? (§4) Does logical inference have further potentials in Recognizing Textual Entailment (RTE) task? and (§5) How efficient is abstract denotation compared to FOL formula? We provide examples or experimental results to the above questions.

*Current affiliation of the first author: Graduate School of Information Sciences, Tohoku University, Japan. Email address: `tianran@ecei.tohoku.ac.jp`

Proceedings of the ACL 2014 Workshop on Semantic Parsing, pages 71–75,
Baltimore, Maryland USA, June 26 2014.

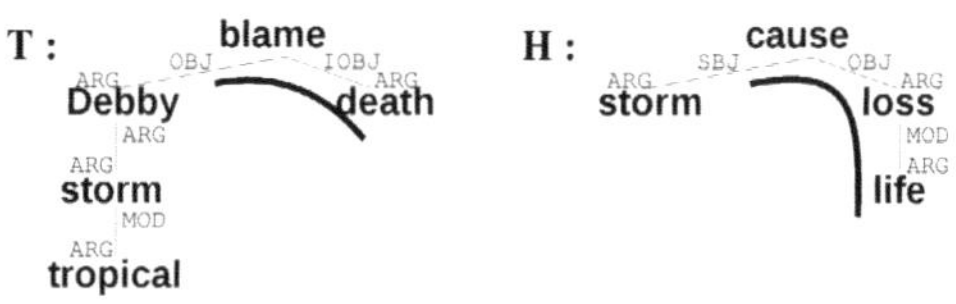

Figure 1: DCS trees of **T:** *Tropical storm Debby is blamed for death* and **H:** *A storm has caused loss of life*

2 Tree transformation vs. logical inference

In the tree transformation based approach to RTE, it has been realized that some gaps between **T** and **H** cannot be filled even by a large number of tree transformation rules extracted from corpus (Bar-Haim et al., 2007a). For example in Figure 1, it is possible to extract the rule *blamed for death* $\rightarrow$ *cause loss of life*, but not easy to extract *tropical storm Debby* $\rightarrow$ *storm*, because "Debby" could be an arbitrary name which may not even appear in the corpus.

This kind of gaps was typically addressed by approximate matching methods, for example by counting common sub-graphs of **T** and **H**, or by computing a cost of tree edits that convert **T** to **H**. In the example of Figure 1, we would expect that **T** is "similar enough" (i.e. has many common sub-graphs) with **H**, or the cost to convert **T** into **H** (e.g. by deleting the node **Debby** and then add the node **storm**) is low. As for how similar is enough, or how the cost is evaluated, we will need a statistical model to train on RTE development set.

It was neglected that some combinations of tree edits are logical (while some are not). The entailment pair in Figure 1 can be easily treated by logical inference, as long as the apposition *tropical storm = Debby* is appropriately handled. In contrast to graph matching or tree edit models which theoretically admit arbitrary tree transformation, logical inference clearly discriminate sound transformations from unsound ones. In this sense, there would be no need to train on RTE data.

When coreference is considered, logically sound tree transformations can be quite complicated. The following is a modified example from RTE2-dev:

T: *Hurricane Isabel, which caused significant damage, was a tropical storm when she entered Virginia.*

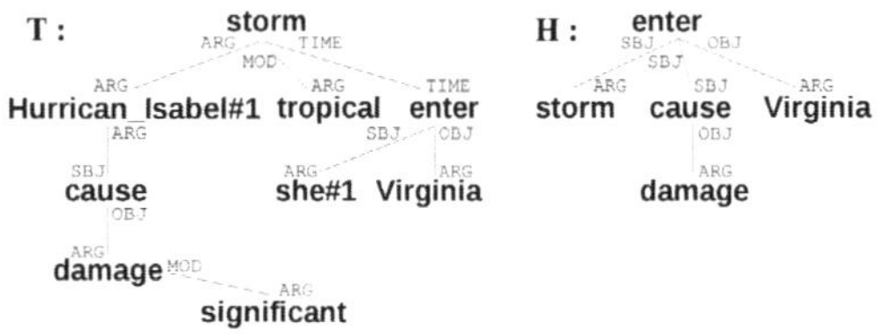

Figure 2: DCS trees with coreference

H: *A storm entered Virginia, causing damage.*

The corresponding DCS trees are shown in Figure 2. Though the DCS trees of **T** and **H** are quite different, **H** can actually be proven from **T**. Note the coreference between *Hurricane Isabel* and *she*, suggesting us to copy the subtree of **Hurricane_Isabel** to **she**, in a tree edit approach. This is not enough yet, because the head **storm** in **T** is not placed at the subject of **cause**. The issue is indeed very logical: from "*Hurricane Isabel = she*", "*Hurricane Isabel = storm*", "*she* = subject of *enter*" and "*Hurricane Isabel* = subject of *cause*", we can imply that "*storm* = subject of *enter* = subject of *cause*".

3 Alignment with logical clues

Tian et al. (2014) proposed a way to generate on-the-fly knowledge to fill knowledge gaps: if **H** is not proven, compare DCS trees of **T** and **H** to generate path alignments (e.g. *blamed for death* $\sim$ *cause loss of life*, as underscored in Figure 1); evaluate the path alignments by a similarity score function; and path alignments with a score greater than a threshold (0.4) are accepted and converted to inference rules.

The word vectors Tian et al. (2014) use to calculate similarities are reported able to capture semantic compositions by simple additions and subtractions (Mikolov et al., 2013). This is also the case when used as knowledge resource for RTE, for example the similarities between **blamed+death** and **cause+loss+life**, or between **found+shot+dead** and **killed**, are computed $>$ 0.4.

However, generally such kind of similarity is very noisy. Tian et al. (2014) used some logical clues to filter out irrelevant path alignments, which helps to keep a high precision. To evaluate the effect of such logical filters, we compare it with some other alignment strategies, the performance of which on RTE5-test data is shown in Table 1.

Each strategy is described in the following.

Strategy	Prec.	Rec.	Acc.
LogicClue + Inference	**69.9**	55.0	**65.7**
LexNoun + Inference	64.2	57.3	62.7
LexNoun + Coverage	57.1	75.0	59.3
NoFilter + Coverage	54.2	**87.7**	56.8

Table 1: Comparison of different alignment strategies

LogicClue + Inference This is the system of Tian et al. (2014)[1], which use logical clues to filter out irrelevant path alignments, and apply accepted path alignments as inference rules.

LexNoun + Inference The same system as above, except that we only align paths between lexically aligned nouns. Two nouns are aligned if and only if they are synonyms, hyponyms or derivatively related in WordNet.

LexNoun + Coverage As above, paths between lexically aligned nouns are aligned, and aligned paths with similarity score > 0.4 are accepted. If all nodes in **H** can be covered by some accepted path alignments, then output "Y". This is very similar to the system described in Bar-Haim et al. (2007b).

NoFilter + Coverage Same as above, but all paths alignments with similarity score > 0.4 are accepted.

4 How can logical inference help RTE?

Logical inference is shown to be useful for RTE, as Tian et al. (2014) demonstrates a system with competitive results. However, despite the expectation that all entailment matters can be explained logically, our observation is that currently logical inference only fills very limited short gaps from **T** to **H**. The logical phenomena easily addressed by Tian et al. (2014)'s framework, namely universal quantifiers and negations, seems rare in PASCAL RTE data. Most heavy lifting is done by distributional similarities between phrases, which may fail in complicated sentences. An especially complex example is:

T: *Wal-Mart Stores Inc. said Tuesday that a Massachusetts judge had granted its motion to decertify a class action lawsuit accusing the world's largest retailer of denying employees breaks.*
H: *Employee breaks had been denied by a motion granted by a Massachusetts judge.*

[1] http://kmcs.nii.ac.jp/tianran/tifmo/

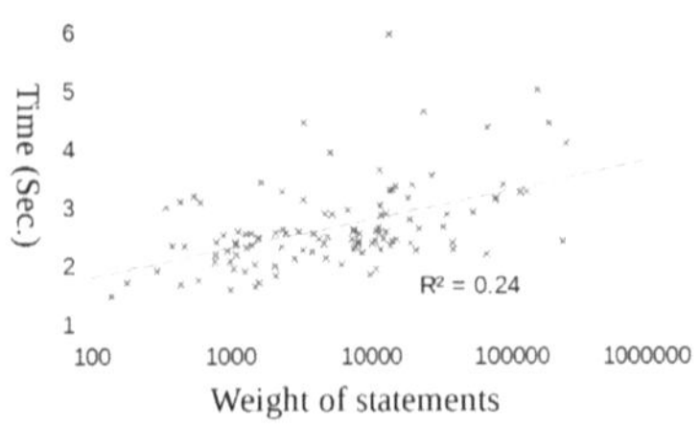

Figure 3: Time of forward-chaining (seconds) in our system, plotted on weights of statements (logarithmic scale).

	Orig. 3 Sec.	Orig. 5 Min.	Red. 5 Min.
Proof found	8	16	82
Too many variables	5	24	3
Failed to find proof	0	1	3
Memory limit	0	2	0
Time out	86	57	13

Table 2: Proportion (%) of exit status of Prover9

The system of Tian et al. (2014) generated on-the-fly knowledge to join several fragments in **T** and wrongly proved **H**. In examples of such complexity, distributional similarity is no longer reliable. However, it may be possible to build a priori logical models at the meta level, such as on epistemic, intentional and reportive attitudes. The models then can provide signals for semantic parsing to connect the logic to natural language, such as the words "*grant*", "*decertify*", and "*accuse*" in the above example. We hope this approach can bring new progress to RTE and other semantic processing tasks.

5 Efficiency of abstract denotations

To evaluate the efficiency of logical inference on abstract denotations, we took 110 true entailment pairs from RTE5 development set, which are also pairs that can be proven with on-the-fly knowledge. We plot the running time of Tian et al. (2014)'s inference engine (single-threaded) on a 2.27GHz Xeon CPU, with respect to the weighted sum of all statements[2], as shown in Figure 3. The graph shows all pairs can be proven in 6 seconds, and proof time scales *logarithmically* on weight of statements.

On the other hand, we converted statements on abstract denotations into FOL formulas, and tried to prove the same pairs using Prover9,[3] a popu-

[2] If a statement is translated to FOL formula, the weight of this statement equals to the weighted sum of all predicates in the FOL formula, where an n-ary predicate is weighted as n.

[3] www.cs.unm.edu/~mccune/prover9/

lar FOL theorem prover. As the result turns out (Table 2), only 8% of the pairs can be proven in 3 seconds (the "Orig. 3 Sec." column), and only 16% pairs can be proven in 5 minutes (the "Orig. 5 Min." column), showing severe difficulties for an FOL prover to handle textual inferences with many (usually hundreds of) on-the-fly rules. As such, we use Tian et al. (2014)'s inference engine to pin down statements that are actually needed for proving **H** (usually just 2 or 3 statements), and try to prove **H** by Prover9 again, using only necessary statements. Proven pairs in 5 minutes then jump to 82% (the "Red. 5 Min." column), showing that a large number of on-the-fly rules may drastically increase computation cost. Still, nearly 20% pairs cannot be proven even in this setting, suggesting that traditional FOL prover is not suited for textual inference.

6 Conclusion and future work

We have discussed the role that logical inference could play in RTE task, and the efficiency of performing inference on abstract denotations. Though currently logical inference contributes at places that are somehow inconspicuous, there is the possibility that with some meta level logical models and the methodology of semantic parsing, we can build systems that understand natural language texts deeply: logic implies (in)consistency, which is in turn used as signals to produce more accurate semantic interpretation. And after all, as there may be many possible variations of semantic representations, it is good to have an efficient inference framework that has the potential to connect them. It would be exciting if we can combine different types of structured data with natural language in semantic processing tasks. Directions of our future work are described below.

Improvement of similarity score To calculate phrase similarities, Tian et al. (2014) use the cosine similarity of sums of word vectors, which ignores syntactic information. We plan to add syntactic information to words by some supertags, and learn a vector space embedding for this structure.

Integration of FreeBase to RTE It would be exciting if we can utilize the huge amount of FreeBase data in RTE task. Using the framework of abstract denotation, meanings of sentences can be explained as relational database queries; to convert it to FreeBase data queries is like relational to ontology schema matching. In order to make effective use of FreeBase data, we also need to recognize entities and relations in natural language sentences. Previous research on semantic parsing will be very helpful for learning such mapping.

Winograd Schema Challenge (WSC) As the RTE task, WSC (Levesque et al., 2012) also provides a test bed for textual inference systems. A Winograd schema is a pair of similar sentences but contain an ambiguity of pronouns that is resolved in opposite ways. A complicated partial example is:

> *Michael decided to freeze himself in cryo-stasis even though his father was against it, because he hopes to be unfrozen in the future when there is a cure available.*

The logical interplay among *decided*, *hopes*, *even though*, *because*, and the realization that *he* is coreferent to *Michael* (but not *his father*) is intriguing. By working on the task, we hope to gain further understanding on how knowledge can be gathered and applied in natural language reasoning.

Acknowledgments This research was supported by the Todai Robot Project at National Institute of Informatics.

References

Roy Bar-Haim, Ido Dagan, Iddo Greental, and Eyal Shnarch. 2007a. Semantic inference at the lexical-syntactic level. In *Proceedings of AAAI 2007*.

Roy Bar-Haim, Ido Dagan, Iddo Greental, Idan Szpektor, and Moshe Friedman. 2007b. Semantic inference at the lexical-syntactic level for textual entailment recognition. In *Proceedings of the ACL-PASCAL Workshop on Textual Entailment and Paraphrasing*.

Hector Levesque, Ernest Davis, and Leora Morgenstern. 2012. The winograd schema challenge. In *Knowledge Representation and Reasoning Conference*.

Percy Liang, Michael Jordan, and Dan Klein. 2011. Learning dependency-based compositional semantics. In *Proceedings of ACL 2011*.

Tomas Mikolov, Wen-tau Yih, and Geoffrey Zweig. 2013. Linguistic regularities in continuous space word representations. In *Proceedings of NAACL 2013*.

Ran Tian, Yusuke Miyao, and Matsuzaki Takuya. 2014. Logical inference on dependency-based compositional semantics. In *Proceedings of ACL 2014*.

Towards README-EVAL : Interpreting README File Instructions

James Paul White
Department of Linguistics
University of Washington
Seattle WA 98195-4340
jimwhite@uw.edu

Abstract

This abstract describes README-EVAL, a novel measure for semantic parsing evaluation of interpreters for instructions in computer program README files. That is enabled by leveraging the tens of thousands of Open Source Software programs that have been annotated by package maintainers of GNU/Linux operating systems. We plan to make available a public shared implementation of this evaluation.

1 Introduction

That natural language is learned by humans in rich grounded perceptual contexts has been recognized by many researchers for quite some time (Regier, 1996) (Silberer and Lapata, 2012). But most efforts at machine learning of natural language continue to address tasks which are entirely divorced from any grounding and/or have perceptual requirements for which machines are ill-suited. Computers are machines and their natural perceptual context is that of the computing machine world. Therefore, to apply the model of grounded language learning most effectively, we should choose tasks in which the relevant percepts are of those in the computing world (e.g., bits, bytes, characters, files, memory, operations, programs, events, processes, services, devices, processors, drivers, operating systems, and networks).

This abstract describes proposed work aimed at the goal of deep semantic parsing of the web, which for us includes the ability to interpret documents that give instructions for acting on computer systems in human natural language. To facilitate research in that direction, we plan to evaluate systems that build software packages by following the README[1] file instructions contained in GNU/Linux distributions like Centos and Debian. Key to this plan is the novel README-EVAL score which we propose as an extrinsic (i.e. goal-oriented) performance measure for parsing, mapping/planning, and related linguistics tasks. The planned baseline system is a pipeline using a document classifier and instruction sequence extractor trained on hand-labeled data followed by a reinforcement learner for mapping the instructions to a build script (plan of actions) for that software package (context).

2 Background

A significant challenge for semantic parsing research is finding a method to measure a system's performance that will indicate its effectiveness in the domain of interest. Traditionally the approach has been to gather and have human annotators make judgements that are of the same kind the system is intended to perform. That process is relatively costly and may result in a corpus which is actually too small considering the amount of variation that occurs when humans perform an activity. Relevant prior work in the computing domain produced the Linux and Monroe plan corpora (Blaylock and Allen, 2005). The Linux Plan Corpus consists of 457 interactive shell script sessions, with an average of 6.1 actions each, captured from human experimental subjects attempting to satisfy one of 19 different goals stated as an English sentence. Although it has been used successfully by those and other researchers, the natural variation in human behavior means that a corpus of such relatively small size appears to be very noisy. As a result they have had to rely on artificially generated data such as the Monroe Plan Corpus in order to get results that are more easily compared across system evaluations.

[1] We use the term README file in a broad sense meaning a document that contains instructions to be read by a human that concern performing actions on a computer (whether at the keyboard or some other input device). For this task we confine ourselves to instructions given for the purpose of building a software package.

Proceedings of the ACL 2014 Workshop on Semantic Parsing, pages 76–81,
Baltimore, Maryland USA, June 26 2014.

More promising therefore is the way some researchers have discovered ways to repurpose data and/or judgements created for other purposes and turn them into training data and/or evaluations of NLP systems. We employ that paradigm here by repurposing the efforts of Open Source Software (OSS) package maintainers who have created annotations (aka metadata) including dependency relations and scripts that build computer programs.

3 GNU/Linux Software Package Data

The advent of the Internet resulted in explosive growth for OSS, the premier example of which is the GNU/Linux operating system family. Current distributions contain packages built from over 15,000 program source bundles.[2] The production of OSS packages for such systems typically involves two different types of programmers working independently. The authors of the source computer program usually do not produce packaging metadata for their work and instead tend to write README files and related documentation explaining how to build and use the software. The package maintainers then work out the specific requirements and scripts necessary to build the program as some package(s) using the particular package manager and format of the OS distribution (aka "distro") that they are supporting. Software package metadata contained in bundles such as Debian `.deb` and Fedora RPM `.spec` files are rich in annotations.[3,4]

See Figure 1 for excerpts of text describing the Bean Scripting Framework (BSF) from its Source RPM Package Manager (SRPM) package in the Fedora Core 17 distribution.[5] The two kinds of data shown are file contents (1a, 1c, 1e), which usually originate with the "upstream" program author(s), and sections from the RPM Spec file (1b, 1d, 1f), which are annotations (aka metadata) curated by the package maintainers. There are other sections and fields used in RPM Spec files, but those tend to more distro-specific and these suffice for this discussion.

Figure 1a shows some BSF package description text from the source README.txt file and Figure 1b shows the version appearing the RPM Spec. That close textual similarity is a common occurrence in the data and can be used to identify some likely README files. Those are only a starting point though, because the natural language program build instructions are often in other files, as in this case. For many packages those instructions are in a file named INSTALL. There is an INSTALL.txt file with some instructions for BSF here (Figure 1e), but they are for a binary installation. The instructions for building from source that we will primarily concerned with here are in the file BUILDING.txt (Figure 1c).

A potential use for this data that we haven't explored yet is its use in summarization tasks. In addition to the text which is usually in the README file and RPM Spec DESCRIPTION section, there is the "Summary" field of the PACKAGE section. Although in Figure 1d the value for the summary field appears as just the package's full name, this is typically a full sentence that is a good one-line summary of the multiple line description section.

It is worthwhile to notice that thousands of programs have been packaged multiple times for different systems (e.g. Debian, Fedora, Cygwin, NixOS, Homebrew, and others) and many packages have also been internationalized.[6] Both of those aspects point to opportunities for learning from parallel data.

For the present discussion we focus on two particular elements of package metadata: dependencies and build scripts.[7] The packages in a distribution have dependency relationships which designate which packages must be built and installed for other packages to be built, installed, and/or executed. These relationships form a directed acyclic graph (DAG) in which the nodes are packages and the edges are dependency relationships.

[2] Debian Wheezy has over 37,000 packages from about 17,500 source packages `https://www.debian.org/News/2013/20130504` and Fedora 20 has more than 15,000 packages `https://admin.fedoraproject.org/pkgdb/collections/`.

[3] `https://www.debian.org/doc/manuals/maint-guide/dreq.en.html`

[4] `http://www.rpm.org/max-rpm/ch-rpm-inside.html`

[5] For more examples, we refer the interested reader the author's web page which includes access to a web linked data explorer for the entire corpus. `http://students.washington.edu/jimwhite/sp14.html`

[6] Debian for example currently lists more than 800k sentences in the localization database and about 75 human languages have translations for at least 100k of them with the top ten languages having over 500k each `https://www.debian.org/international/l10n/po/rank`.

[7] Packaging systems usually support at least three types of scripts: build, install, and remove. The build script usually has more in common with the README instructions than the install and remove scripts which are more distro specific. Some packages also have a check script to validate the state of a build prior to performing the install operation.

(a) README.txt file

Bean Scripting Framework (BSF) is a set of Java classes which provides an easy to use scripting language support within Java applications. It also provides access to Java objects and methods from supported scripting languages.
...

(b) RPM Spec DESCRIPTION section

Bean Scripting Framework (BSF) is a set of Java classes which provides scripting language support within Java applications, and access to Java objects and methods from scripting languages.
...

(c) BUILDING.txt file

```
From the ant "build.xml" file:
  Master Build file for BSF
Notes:
  This is the build file for use with
  the Jakarta Ant build tool.
Optional additions:
 BeanShell -> http://www.beanshell.org/
 Jython -> http://www.jython.org/
 JRuby -> http://www.jruby.org/ (3rd ...)
 Xalan -> http://xml.apache.org/xalan-j
 ...
Build Instructions:
 To build, run
  java org.apache.tools.ant.Main <target>
 on the directory where this file is
 located with the target you want.
Most useful targets:
- all -> creates the binary and src
 distributions, and builds the site
- compile -> creates the "bsf.jar"
 package in "./build/lib" (default target)
- samples -> creates/compiles the samples
...
```

(d) RPM Spec PACKAGE section (metadata)

```
Name:           bsf
Version:        2.4.0
Release:        12.fc17
Summary:        Bean Scripting Framework
License:        ASL 2.0
URL:     http://commons.apache.org/bsf/
Group:          Development/Libraries
BuildRequires: jpackage-utils >= 1.6
BuildRequires: ant, xalan-j2, jython
BuildRequires: rhino
BuildRequires: apache-commons-logging
Requires:       xalan-j2
Requires:       apache-commons-logging
Requires:       jpackage-utils
BuildArch:      noarch
...
```

(e) INSTALL.txt file

```
Installing BSF consists of copying
bsf.jar and .jars for any languages
intended to be supported to a directory
in the execution CLASSPATH of your
application, or simply adding them
to your CLASSPATH.
BSF can be used either as a standalone
system, as a class library, or as part
of an application server. In order to be
used as a class library or as a standalone
system, one must simply download the
bsf.jar file from the BSF web site
(http://jakarta.apache.org/bsf/index.html)
and include it in their CLASSPATH, along
with any required classes or jar files
implementing the desired languages.
...
```

(f) RPM Spec BUILD section (shell script)

```
[ -z "$JAVA_HOME" ] && export JAVA_HOME=/usr/lib/jvm/java
export CLASSPATH=$(build-classpath apache-commons-logging jython xalan-j2 rhino)
ant jar
/usr/bin/rm -rf bsf/src/org/apache/bsf/engines/java
ant javadocs
```

Figure 1: Bean Scripting Framework (BSF) excerpts from Fedora Core 17 RPMS.

4 From Dependencies to Validation

The idea that turns the package dependency DAG into training, test, and evaluation data is to choose dependency targets for test (i.e. the system build script outputs will be used for them in test) and dependency sources (the dependent packages) for validation (their package maintainer written build scripts are used as is to observe whether the dependencies are likely to be good). Validation subsets can be arranged for both internal validation (tuning) and external validation (evaluation).

Two kinds of dependency relationships are of special interest here: `Requires` and `BuildRequires`. The former typically means the target package (its name appears to the right of a `Requires` or `BuildRequires` in Figure 1d) is required at both build time and execution time by the source package (identified by the `Name` field of Figure 1d) while the latter means it is only required at build time. That distinction can be used to guide the selection of which packages to choose for the validation and test subsets. Packages that are the target of a `BuildRequires` relationship are more likely to cause their dependents' build scripts to fail when they (the targets) are built incorrectly than targets of a `Requires` relationship.

Analysis of the 2,121 packages in Release 17 of the Fedora Core SRPM distribution shows 1,673 package nodes that have a build script and some declared dependency relationship. Those build scripts average 6.9 non-blank lines each. Of those nodes, 1,009 are leaves and the 664 internal nodes are the target of an average of 7 dependencies each. There are 218 internal nodes that are the direct target of at least one leaf node via a `BuildRequires` relationship and they average 12.4 such dependent leaves each. We expect to have a larger corpus prepared from a full GNU/Linux distribution (at least 15,000 source packages) at the time of the workshop.

5 Task Description

The top-level README-EVAL task would be to generate complete packaging metadata given the source files for a program thus automating the work of a package maintainer. Since that task is somewhat complicated, it is useful to break it down into multiple subtasks which can be addressed and evaluated separately before proceeding to combine them. For the discussion here we will consider a partial solution using a four stage pipeline: README document classification, instruction extraction, dependency relation extraction, and build script generation.

The corpus' package metadata can be used to directly evaluate the results of the last two stages of that pipeline. The first two stages, README document classification and instruction extraction, are well understood tasks for which a moderate amount of manually labelled data can suffice to train and test effective classifiers.

The dependency relation extraction subtask can be treated as a conventional information extraction task concerned with named entity recognition for packages and relation extraction for dependencies. We may regard the dependencies in the corpus as effectively canonical because the package maintainers strive to keep those annotations to a reasonable minimum. Therefore computing precision and recall scores of the dependency DAG edges and labels of this stage's output versus the corpus' metadata will be a meaningful metric.

Work on instruction and direction following is applicable to the build script generation subtask. Such systems tend to be somewhat more complex than shallow extraction systems and may incorporate further subcomponents including goal detectors and/or planners that interact with a semantic parser (Branavan et al., 2012). It is possible to evaluate the final stage output by comparing it to the build script in the package's metadata, but that would suffer from the same sort of evaluation problems that other language generation tasks have when we are concerned with semantics rather than syntax. This is where the superiority of an NLP task where the target language is understood by computers comes in, because we can also evaluate it using execution. Which isn't to say we can solve the program equivalence problem in general, but README-EVAL does a pragmatic determination of how good a substitute it is based on its usage by the package's dependency sources.

6 README-EVAL Scoring

The README-EVAL score is a measure of how effective the system under test (SUT) is at generating software package metadata. For the components of the SUT this score can serve as an extrinsic indication of their effectiveness.

Let N be a set of tuples (x, y) representing the corpus in which x is the package data and relevant metadata subset minus the labels to be generated and y is a known good label for x. To prepare the corpus for the task, two disjoint subsets C and T are selected from the set of all package nodes N. C is for the common packages which are available to the SUT for training, and T is for the test packages that the SUT's interpretation function will be tested on. A third set V which is disjoint from T is selected from N for the validation packages.

Many partitioning schemes are possible. A simple method is to choose the leaf nodes (packages that are sources but not targets of dependency relationships) for V. The members of T can then be chosen as the set of packages which are the direct targets of the dependency relationships from V. The members of V are expected to be likely to fail to build correctly if there are errors in the system outputs for T. Note that for the SUT to do tuning it will need some leaf node packages in C. Therefore if V is made disjoint from C then it should not actually select all of those leaves.

The README-EVAL score R is computed using a suitable loss function L for the SUT's label predictor function $\hat{Y}$. $\hat{Y}$ is presumed to have been trained on C and it yields a set of $(x, \hat{y})$ tuples given a set of x values. The loss function $L((x, y), D)$ yields a real number in the range 0 to 1 inclusive that indicates what fraction of the components in package (x, y) are incorrect given the context $D \subset N$. It is required for all $v \in V$ that $L(v, (C \cup T \cup V) \setminus \{v\}) = 0$.

For this exposition, assume y is a build script and L yields 0 if it succeeds and 1 if it fails. Linux processes typically indicate success by returning a zero exit code. Therefore a simple realization of

L is to return 0 if the process executing the build script y of (x, y) given D returns zero and 1 otherwise.

The computation iterates over each member $D \in partition(T)$ and obtains measures of correctness by evaluating $B(\hat{Y}(X(D)) \cup C \cup T \setminus D)$ where X is a function that yields the set of x values for a given set of (x, y) tuples. To keep the task as easy as possible, the members of $partition(T)$ may be singletons.

$B(D) = |V| - \sum_{v \in V} L(v, (D \cup V) \setminus \{v\})$

Those values are normalized by a scale factor for each D determined by the value of B given D minus B given $Z(D)$. $Z(D)$ is the set of tuples (x, λ) for a given set D where λ is the null label. A null label for a build script is one which has no actions and executes successfully.

$R(D) = \frac{B(\hat{Y}(X(D)) \cup C \cup T \setminus D)}{B(C \cup T) - B(Z(D) \cup C \cup T \setminus D)}$

The final README-EVAL measure R is the average score over those partitions:

$R = \frac{\sum_{D \in partition(T)} R(D)}{|partition(T)|}$

6.1 Loss Function Variations

There are other useful implementation variations for the loss function L. In a system where the number of components can be determined independently from whether they are correct or not, a possibly superior alternative is to return the number of incorrect components divided by the total number of components. To determine loss for a build script for example, the value may be determined by counting the number of actions that execute successfully and dividing by the total number of steps.

A further consideration in semantic evaluation is parsimony, which is the general expectation that the shortest adequate solution is to be preferred (Gagne et al., 2006). To incorporate parsimony in the evaluation we can add a measure(s) of the solution's cost(s), such as the size of the label y and/or execution resources consumed, to L.

7 Conclusion

A common objection to tackling this task is that it seems too hard given the state of our knowledge about human language, computer programming (as performed by humans), and especially the capabilities of current NLP systems. We consider that to be a feature rather than a bug. It may be some time before a state-of-the-art implementation of a README interpreter is sufficiently capable to be considered comparable to an expert human GNU/Linux package maintainer performance, but that is perfectly fine because we would like to have an evaluation that is robust, long-lived, and applicable to many NLP subtasks. We also have the more pragmatic response given here which shows that that difficult task can be decomposed into smaller subtasks like others that have been addressed in the NLP and computational linguistics communities.

To conclude, this proposal recommends README-EVAL as an extrinsic (goal-oriented) evaluation system for semantic parsing that could provide a meaningful indication of performance for a variety of NLP components.

Because the evaluation platform may be somewhat complicated to set up and run, we would like to make a publicly available shared evaluation platform on which it would be a simple matter to submit new systems or components for evaluation. The MLcomp.org system developed by Percy Liang and Jacob Abernethy, a free website for objectively comparing machine learning programs, is an especially relevant precedent (Gollub et al., 2012). But we notice that the NLP tasks on MLcomp receive little activity (the last new run was more than a year ago at this writing) which is in stark contrast to the other ML tasks which are very active (as they are on sites like Kaggle). With the README-EVAL task available in such an easy-to-use manner could draw significant participation because of its interesting and challenging domain, especially from ML and other CS students and researchers.

Finally we look forward to discussing this proposal with the workshop attendees, particularly in working out the details for manual annotation of the README files for the instruction extractor (including whether it is needed), and discussing ideas for a baseline implementation.

8 Acknowledgements

Thank you to my University of Washington colleagues who reviewed earlier drafts of this abstract and the workshop's blind reviewers for their helpful comments.

References

Nate Blaylock and James Allen. 2005. Recognizing Instantiated Goals using Statistical Methods. In *IJCAI Workshop on Modeling Others from Observations (MOO-2005)*, page 79.

S. R. K. Branavan, Nate Kushman, Tao Lei, and Regina Barzilay. 2012. Learning High-Level Planning from Text. In *Proceedings of the 50th Annual Meeting of the Association for Computational Linguistics: Long Papers-Volume 1*, page 126. Association for Computational Linguistics.

Christian Gagne, Marc Schoenauer, Marc Parizeau, and Marco Tomassini. 2006. Genetic Programming, Validation Sets, and Parsimony Pressure. In *Genetic Programming*, page 109. Springer.

Tim Gollub, Benno Stein, and Steven Burrows. 2012. Ousting Ivory Tower Research: Towards a Web Framework for Providing Experiments as a Service. In *Proceedings of the 35th international ACM SIGIR conference on Research and development in information retrieval*, page 1125. ACM.

Terry Regier. 1996. *The Human Semantic Potential: Spatial Language and Constrained Connectionism*. MIT Press.

Carina Silberer and Mirella Lapata. 2012. Grounded Models of Semantic Representation. In *Proceedings of the 2012 Joint Conference on Empirical Methods in Natural Language Processing and Computational Natural Language Learning*, page 1423. Association for Computational Linguistics.

Freebase QA: Information Extraction or Semantic Parsing?

Xuchen Yao [1] **Jonathan Berant** [3] **Benjamin Van Durme** [1,2]
[1]Center for Language and Speech Processing
[2]Human Language Technology Center of Excellence
Johns Hopkins University
[3]Computer Science Department
Stanford University

Abstract

We contrast two seemingly distinct approaches to the task of question answering (QA) using Freebase: one based on information extraction techniques, the other on semantic parsing. Results over the same test-set were collected from two state-of-the-art, open-source systems, then analyzed in consultation with those systems' creators. We conclude that the differences between these technologies, both in task performance, and in how they get there, is not significant. This suggests that the semantic parsing community should target answering more compositional open-domain questions that are beyond the reach of more direct information extraction methods.

1 Introduction

Question Answering (QA) from structured data, such as DBPedia (Auer et al., 2007), Freebase (Bollacker et al., 2008) and Yago2 (Hoffart et al., 2011), has drawn significant interest from both knowledge base (KB) and semantic parsing (SP) researchers. The majority of such work treats the KB as a database, to which standard database queries (SPARQL, MySQL, etc.) are issued to retrieve answers. Language understanding is modeled as the task of converting natural language questions into queries through intermediate logical forms, with the popular two approaches including: CCG parsing (Zettlemoyer and Collins, 2005; Zettlemoyer and Collins, 2007; Zettlemoyer and Collins, 2009; Kwiatkowski et al., 2010; Kwiatkowski et al., 2011; Krishnamurthy and Mitchell, 2012; Kwiatkowski et al., 2013; Cai and Yates, 2013a), and dependency-based compositional semantics (Liang et al., 2011; Berant et al., 2013; Berant and Liang, 2014).

We characterize semantic parsing as the task of deriving a representation of meaning from language, sufficient for a given task. Traditional information extraction (IE) from text may be coarsely characterized as representing a certain level of semantic parsing, where the goal is to derive enough meaning in order to populate a database with factoids of a form matching a given schema.[1] Given the ease with which reasonably accurate, deep syntactic structure can be automatically derived over (English) text, it is not surprising that IE researchers would start including such "features" in their models.

Our question is then: what is the difference between an IE system with access to syntax, as compared to a semantic parser, when both are targeting a factoid-extraction style task? While our conclusions should hold generally for similar KBs, we will focus on Freebase, such as explored by Krishnamurthy and Mitchell (2012), and then others such as Cai and Yates (2013a) and Berant et al. (2013). We compare two open-source, state-of-the-art systems on the task of Freebase QA: the semantic parsing system SEMPRE (Berant et al., 2013), and the IE system jacana-freebase (Yao and Van Durme, 2014).

We find that these two systems are on par with each other, with no significant differences in terms of accuracy between them. A major distinction between the work of Berant et al. (2013) and Yao and Van Durme (2014) is the ability of the former to represent, and compose, aggregation operators (such as `argmax`, or `count`), as well as integrate disparate pieces of information. This representational capability was important in previous, closed-domain tasks such as GeoQuery. The move to Freebase by the SP community was meant to

[1] So-called Open Information Extraction (OIE) is simply a further blurring of the distinction between IE and SP, where the schema is allowed to grow with the number of verbs, and other predicative elements of the language.

Proceedings of the ACL 2014 Workshop on Semantic Parsing, pages 82–86,
Baltimore, Maryland USA, June 26 2014.

provide richer, open-domain challenges. While the vocabulary increased, our analysis suggests that compositionality and complexity decreased. We therefore conclude that the semantic parsing community should target more challenging open-domain datasets, ones that "standard IE" methods are less capable of attacking.

2 IE and SP Systems

jacana-freebase[2] (Yao and Van Durme, 2014) treats QA from a KB as a binary classification problem. Freebase is a gigantic graph with millions of nodes (topics) and billions of edges (relations). For each question, jacana-freebase first selects a "view" of Freebase concerning only involved topics and their close neighbors (this "view" is called a topic graph). For instance, for the question "who is the brother of justin bieber?", the topic graph of Justin Bieber, containing all related nodes to the topic (think of the "Justin Bieber" page displayed by the browser), is selected and retrieved by the Freebase Topic API. Usually such a topic graph contains hundreds to thousands of nodes in close relation to the central topic. Then each of the node is judged as answer or not by a logistic regression learner.

Features for the logistic regression learner are first extracted from both the question and the topic graph. An analysis of the dependency parse of the question characterizes the question word, topic, verb, and named entities of the main subject as the question features, such as qword=who. Features on each node include the types of relations and properties the node possesses, such as type=person. Finally features from both the question and each node are combined as the final features used by the learner, such as qword=who|type=person. In this way the association between the question and answer type is enforced. Thus during decoding, for instance, if there is a who question, the nodes with a person property would be ranked higher as the answer candidate.

SEMPRE[3] is an open-source system for training semantic parsers, that has been utilized to train a semantic parser against Freebase by Berant et al. (2013). SEMPRE maps NL utterances to logical forms by performing bottom-up parsing. First, a lexicon is used to map NL phrases to KB predicates, and then predicates are combined to form a full logical form by a context-free grammar. Since logical forms can be derived in multiple ways from the grammar, a log-linear model is used to rank possible derivations. The parameters of the model are trained from question-answer pairs.

[2]`https://code.google.com/p/jacana/`

[3]`http://www-nlp.stanford.edu/software/sempre/`

3 Analysis

3.1 Evaluation Metrics

Both Berant et al. (2013) and Yao and Van Durme (2014) tested their systems on the WEBQUESTIONS dataset, which contains 3778 training questions and 2032 test questions collected from the Google Suggest API. Each question came with a standard answer from Freebase annotated by Amazon Mechanical Turk.

Berant et al. (2013) reported a score of 31.4% in terms of accuracy (with partial credit if inexact match) on the test set and later in Berant and Liang (2014) revised it to 35.7%. Berant et al. focused on accuracy – how many questions were correctly answered by the system. Since their system answered almost all questions, accuracy is roughly identical to F_1. Yao and Van Durme (2014)'s system on the other hand only answered 80% of all test questions. Thus they report a score of 42% in terms of F_1 on this dataset. For the purpose of comparing among *all* test questions, we lowered the logistic regression prediction threshold (usually 0.5) on jacana-freebase for the other 20% of questions where jacana-freebase had not proposed an answer to, and selected the best-possible prediction with the highest prediction score as the answer. In this way jacana-freebase was able to answer all questions with a lower accuracy of 35.4%. In the following we present analysis results based on the test questions where the two systems had very similar performance (35.7% vs. 35.4%).[4] The difference is not significant according to the paired permutation test (Smucker et al., 2007).

3.2 Accuracy vs. Coverage

First, we were interested to see the proportions of questions SEMPRE and jacana-freebase jointly and separately answered correctly. The answer to

[4]In this setting accuracy equals averaged macro F_1: first the F_1 value on each question were computed, then averaged among all questions, or put it in other words: "accuracy with partial credit". In this section our usage of the terms "accuracy" and "F_1" can be exchanged.

		jacana ($F_1 = 1$)		jacana ($F_1 \geq 0.5$)	
		$\surd$	$\times$	$\surd$	$\times$
SEMPRE	$\surd$	153 (0.08)	383 (0.19)	429 (0.21)	321 (0.16)
	$\times$	136 (0.07)	1360 (0.67)	366 (0.18)	916 (0.45)

Table 1: The absolute and proportion of questions SEMPRE and jacana-freebase answered correctly ($\surd$) and incorrectly ($\times$) jointly and separately, running a threshold F_1 of 1 and 0.5.

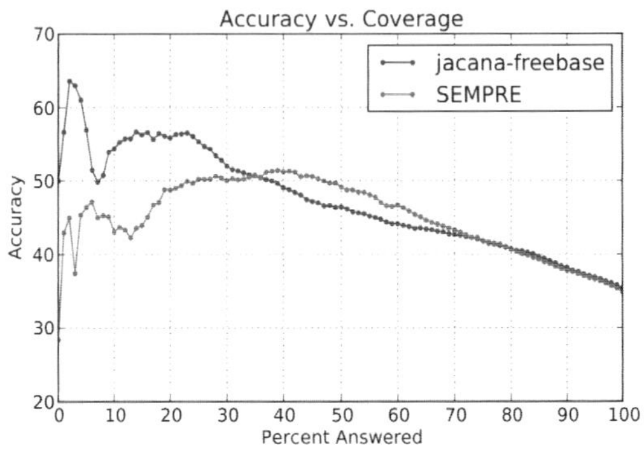

Figure 1: Precision with respect to proportion of questions answered

many questions in the dataset is a set of answers, for example what to see near sedona arizona?. Since turkers did not exhaustively pick out all possible answers, evaluation is performed by computing the F_1 between the set of answers given by the system and the answers provided by turkers. With a strict threshold of $F_1 = 1$ and a permissive threshold of $F_1 \geq 0.5$ to judge the correctness, we list the pair-wise correctness matrix in Table 1. Not surprisingly, both systems had most questions wrong given that the averaged F_1's were only around 35%. With the threshold $F_1 = 1$, SEMPRE answered more questions exactly correctly compared to jacana-freebase, while when $F_1 \geq 0.5$, it was the other way around. This shows that SEMPRE is more accurate in certain questions. The reason behind this is that SEMPRE always fires queries that return exactly one set of answers from Freebase, while jacana-freebase could potentially tag multiple nodes as the answer, which may lower the accuracy.

We have shown that both systems can be more accurate in certain questions, but when? Is there a correlation between the system confidence and accuracy? Thus we took the logistic decoding score (between 0 and 1) from jacana-freebase and the probability from the log-linear model used by SEMPRE as confidence, and plotted an "accuracy vs. coverage" curve, which shows the accuracy of a QA engine with respect to its coverage of all questions. The curve basically answers one question: at a fixed accuracy, what is the proportion of questions that can be answered? A better system should be able to answer more questions correctly with the same accuracy.

The curve was drawn in the following way. For each question, we select the best answer candidate with the highest confidence score. Then for the whole test set, we have a list of (question, highest ranked answer, confidence score) tuples. Running a threshold from 1 to 0, we select those questions with an answer confidence score above the threshold and compute accuracy at this point. The X-axis indicates the percentage of questions above the threshold and the Y-axis the accuracy, shown in Figure 1.

The two curves generally follow a similar trend, but while jacana-freebase has higher accuracy when coverage is low, SEMPRE obtains slightly better accuracy when more questions are answered.

3.3 Accuracy by Question Length and Type

Do accuracies of the two systems differ with respect to the complexity of questions? Since there is no clear way to measure question complexity, we use question length as a surrogate and report accuracies by question length in Figure 2. Most of the questions were 5 to 8 words long and there was no substantial difference in terms of accuracies. The major difference lies in questions of length 3, 12 and 13. However, the number of such questions was not high enough to show any statistical significance.

Figure 3 further shows the accuracies with respect to the question types (as reflected by the WH-word). Again, there is no significant difference between the two systems.

3.4 Learned Features

What did the systems learn during training? We compare them by presenting the top features by weight, as listed in Table 2. Clearly, the type of knowledge learned by the systems in these features is similar: both systems learn to associate certain phrases with predicates from the KB.

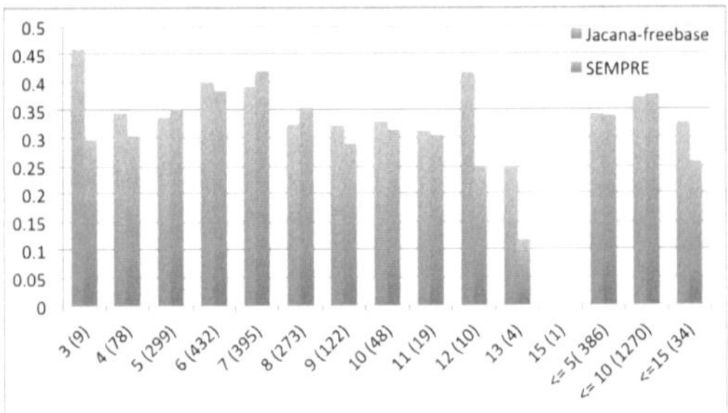

Figure 2: Accuracy (Y-axis) by question length. The X-axis specifies the question length in words and the total number of questions in parenthesis.

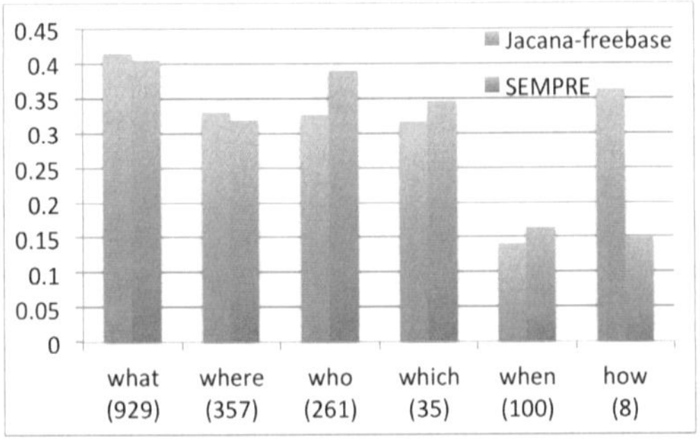

Figure 3: Accuracy by question type (and the number of questions).

We note, however, that SEMPRE also obtains information from the fully constructed logical form. For instance, SEMPRE learns that logical forms that return an empty set when executed against the KB are usually incorrect (the weight for this feature is -8.88). In this respect the SP approach "understands" more than the IE approach.

We did not further compare on other datasets such as GeoQuery (Tang and Mooney, 2001) and FREE917 (Cai and Yates, 2013b). The first one involves geographic inference and multiple contraints in queries, directly fitting the compositional nature of semantic parsing. The second one was manually generated by looking at Freebase topics. Both datasets were less realistic than the WEBQUESTIONS dataset. Both datasets were also less challenging (accuracy/F_1 were between 80% and 90%) compared to WEBQUESTIONS (around 40%).

4 Discussion and Conclusion

Our analysis of two QA approaches, semantic parsing and information extraction, has shown no significant difference between them. Note the similarity between features used in both systems shown in Table 2: the systems learned the same "knowledge" from data, with the distinction that the IE approach acquired this through a direct association between dependency parses and answer properties, while the SP approach acquired this through optimizing on intermediate logic forms.

feature	weight
qfocus=religion|type=Religion	8.60
qfocus=money|type=Currency	5.56
qverb=die|type=CauseOfDeath	5.35
qword=when|type=datetime	5.11
qverb=border|rel=location.adjoins	4.56

(a) jacana-freebase

feature	weight
die from=CauseOfDeath	10.23
die of=CauseOfDeath	7.55
accept=Currency	7.30
bear=PlaceOfBirth	7.11
in switzerland=Switzerland	6.86

(b) SEMPRE

Table 2: Learned top features and their weights for jacana-freebase and SEMPRE.

With a direct information extraction technology easily getting on par with the more sophisticated semantic parsing method, it suggests that SP-based approaches for QA with Freebase has not yet shown its power from a "deeper" understanding of the questions, among questions of various lengths. We suggest that more compositional open-domain datasets should be created, and that SP researchers should focus on utterances in existing datasets that are beyond the reach of direct IE methods.

5 Acknowledgement

We thank the Allen Institute for Artificial Intelligence for assistance in funding this work. This material is partially based on research sponsored by the NSF under grant IIS-1249516 and DARPA under agreements number FA8750-13-2-0017 and FA8750-13-2-0040 (the DEFT program).

References

Sören Auer, Christian Bizer, Georgi Kobilarov, Jens Lehmann, Richard Cyganiak, and Zachary Ives. 2007. DBPedia: A nucleus for a web of open data. In *The semantic web*, pages 722–735. Springer.

Jonathan Berant and Percy Liang. 2014. Semantic parsing via paraphrasing. In *Proceedings of ACL*.

Jonathan Berant, Andrew Chou, Roy Frostig, and Percy Liang. 2013. Semantic Parsing on Freebase from Question-Answer Pairs. In *Proceedings of EMNLP*.

Kurt Bollacker, Colin Evans, Praveen Paritosh, Tim Sturge, and Jamie Taylor. 2008. Freebase: a collaboratively created graph database for structuring human knowledge. In *Proceedings of the 2008 ACM SIGMOD international conference on Management of data*, pages 1247–1250. ACM.

Qingqing Cai and Alexander Yates. 2013a. Large-scale semantic parsing via schema matching and lexicon extension. In *Proceedings of ACL*.

Qingqing Cai and Alexander Yates. 2013b. Large-scale semantic parsing via schema matching and lexicon extension. In *Proceedings of ACL*.

Johannes Hoffart, Fabian M Suchanek, Klaus Berberich, Edwin Lewis-Kelham, Gerard De Melo, and Gerhard Weikum. 2011. Yago2: exploring and querying world knowledge in time, space, context, and many languages. In *Proceedings of the 20th international conference companion on World Wide Web*, pages 229–232. ACM.

Jayant Krishnamurthy and Tom Mitchell. 2012. Weakly supervised training of semantic parsers. In *Proceedings of EMNLP*.

Tom Kwiatkowski, Luke Zettlemoyer, Sharon Goldwater, and Mark Steedman. 2010. Inducing probabilistic CCG grammars from logical form with higher-order unification. In *Proceedings of EMNLP*, pages 1223–1233.

Tom Kwiatkowski, Luke Zettlemoyer, Sharon Goldwater, and Mark Steedman. 2011. Lexical generalization in CCG grammar induction for semantic parsing. In *Proceedings of EMNLP*.

Tom Kwiatkowski, Eunsol Choi, Yoav Artzi, and Luke Zettlemoyer. 2013. Scaling Semantic Parsers with On-the-fly Ontology Matching. In *Proceedings of EMNLP*.

Percy Liang, Michael I. Jordan, and Dan Klein. 2011. Learning Dependency-Based Compositional Semantics. In *Proceedings of ACL*.

M.D. Smucker, J. Allan, and B. Carterette. 2007. A comparison of statistical significance tests for information retrieval evaluation. In *Proceedings of the sixteenth ACM conference on Conference on information and knowledge management*, pages 623–632. ACM.

Lappoon R Tang and Raymond J Mooney. 2001. Using multiple clause constructors in inductive logic programming for semantic parsing. In *Machine Learning: ECML 2001*. Springer.

Xuchen Yao and Benjamin Van Durme. 2014. Information extraction over structured data: Question answering with freebase. In *Proceedings of ACL*.

Luke S Zettlemoyer and Michael Collins. 2005. Learning to map sentences to logical form: Structured classification with probabilistic categorial grammars. *Uncertainty in Artificial Intelligence (UAI)*.

Luke S. Zettlemoyer and Michael Collins. 2007. Online learning of relaxed CCG grammars for parsing to logical form. In *Proceedings of EMNLP-CoNLL*.

Luke S Zettlemoyer and Michael Collins. 2009. Learning context-dependent mappings from sentences to logical form. In *Proceedings of ACL-CoNLL*.

Author Index

Allen, James, 1

Beltagy, Islam, 7
Berant, Jonathan, 82
Beschke, Sebastian, 12
Blunsom, Phil, 22
Bošnjak, Matko, 45

Chang, Angel, 17
Chang, Nancy, 33

Dagan, Ido, 66
de Freitas, Nando, 22
Diamantopoulos, Themistoklis, 50
Dodge, Ellen K, 39

Erk, Katrin, 7

Ficler, Jessica, 66

Goldberg, Yoav, 66
Grefenstette, Edward, 22

Hermann, Karl Moritz, 22

Klein, Ewan, 50

Lewis, Mike, 28
Liu, Yang, 12

Malmaud, Jonathan, 33
Manning, Christopher, 17
Matsuzaki, Takuya, 71
Menzel, Wolfgang, 12
Miyao, Yusuke, 71
Mooney, Raymond, 7
Murphy, Kevin, 33

Petruck, Miriam R L, 39

Riedel, Sebastian, 45
Rocktäschel, Tim, 45
Roth, Michael, 50

Savva, Manolis, 17
Schluter, Natalie, 61
Schubert, Lenhart, 55
Singh, Sameer, 45
Stanovsky, Gabriel, 66
Steedman, Mark, 28
Symeonidis, Andreas, 50

Tian, Ran, 71

Van Durme, Benjamin, 82

Wagner, Earl, 33
White, James, 76

Yao, Xuchen, 82

Association for Computational Linguistics
209 N. Eighth Street
Stroudsburg, Pennsylvania 18360

3rd International Workshop on Computational Terminology

(COMPUTERM 2004)

Held at COLING 2004

Geneva, Switzerland
29 August 2004

ISBN: 978-1-63439-678-3